BISON
BOOKS

D0285765

IN SEARCH OF
POWDER

A STORY OF AMERICA'S
DISAPPEARING SKI BUM

JEREMY EVANS
FOREWORD BY GLEN PLAKE

UNIVERSITY OF NEBRASKA PRESS
LINCOLN AND LONDON

Parts of this book originally appeared
in the *Tahoe Daily Tribune*.

∞

Library of Congress Cataloging-in-
Publication Data

Evans, Jeremy.
In search of powder: a story of
America's disappearing ski bum /
Jeremy Evans; foreword by Glen Plake.
p.   cm.
Includes bibliographical references.
ISBN 978-0-8032-2839-9
(pbk.: alk. paper)
1. Skis and skiing—Social aspects—
United States. 2. Skis and skiing—
United States. 3. Lifestyles—United
States. I. Title.
GV854.9.S63E93   2010
796.930973—dc22
2010004138

Set in Swift by Bob Reitz.

To my wife, Isabelle, whose love has no capacity.

Foreword

GLEN PLAKE

On May 4, 1986, the last day of the ski season at Kirkwood Mountain Resort near Lake Tahoe things were going great for me. I had just returned from my first ski film shoot. After skiing since I was two years old and honing my ski skills basically my entire life, I was going to be in a ski film, which is kind of a weird threshold—a graduation—among skiers. But as I was sharing stories of the film shoot that day with two friends, it happened. While skiing at Kirkwood, a small avalanche knocked me over. I stopped after falling through some rocks. I immediately realized that I had broken my femur. Injuries aren't something we want to happen, but we all know they can. We are skiers—not golfers—and let's face it, skiing can be dangerous.

It was when ski patrol members were cutting my pants to perform medical procedures that one of them discovered my lift ticket—or what I had been using for one. I was approaching two hundred days on the mountain that season, scattered at more than a half dozen ski areas. It was the second winter in a row that I didn't have a season pass to any of them, but I managed to ski whenever I wanted. The techniques to access a ski resort in that way have varied since then—though some still apply—but technology has led to new techniques.

The broken femur kept me off skis for eighteen months, though it healed great. Two years after the injury, in February of 1988, I spent three weeks filming in Chamonix, France, with Greg Stump for his ski film *Blizzard of AAHHH's*. After filming, I was faced with a dilemma. I could either return to California, where I had some unresolved legal issues that happened while I was recovering from my broken leg, or I could trust my skis with my life—both literally and philosophically—like I had done so many times before. The ski pass I had been issued for Greg's film was valid for the rest of the season. I asked myself "What else do I need?"

The decision was made with twenty-three dollars in my pocket. I said au revoir to my friends in California and stayed in Chamonix. I squatted in the judge's tower next to the local ski jump. I picked mountain berries and traded them with a baker, who then provided me my daily bread. I eventually found some odd jobs and did some house-sitting before I returned to the United States almost two years later. Looking back, it was the smarter decision. The time spent in Chamonix helped me become the skier I am today.

Nearly two decades after I made that decision, my wife, Kimberly, and I lived in an RV for almost two months during the 2007 winter. I had been skiing professionally for more than sixteen years, and the previous winter was one of the greatest ever. I climbed and skied from Kullu Pumori, a 22,000-foot peak in the Indian Himalaya, but that was just one of the many highlights of that winter. Kimberly and I traveled through the American Midwest and other areas, calling it our "Down Home Tour." We skied small hills and enjoyed the camaraderie that ski bums enjoy with each other. Some worked jobs so they could volunteer for ski patrol. Others worked as instructors/coaches, lift mechanics, truck drivers, or were students taking a break from classes. They were as diverse as society itself. It is on these hills where the heart of the ski bum may be the biggest.

I believe the ski bum is alive and well and exists in all corners of our world. Some are stationary, some are migrating, but they all are seeking the same goal—ski! Sure, perfect snow in an idyllic setting is a dream, but the real ski bum is simply trying to make skiing an everyday occurrence in their life. I am not talking about the "seasoners," the new college graduates ski bumming for a few years before succumbing to the real world. No, I am talking about the ski bum with a life sentence. Our stories are diverse and as colorful as the days and places we ski. Some of us have fortune and fame, some of us are just getting by, but neither is more important than the other. The "I just want to ski" mentality is the common ground.

In Search of Powder reveals this mentality, taking a close look into the lives of ski bums and their paths along the way, but it also explores some very real situations, especially the habitat of the ski bum. For many, it's like animals having to relocate and readjust due to urban sprawl. The ski bum and the communities they live in are facing real problems, as Jeremy writes in this book. The cost of living in mountain towns has increased so much that the mountain town has become the "mountain resort." Vacation homes have driven up housing costs and have left neighborhoods empty. Employment that once was the domain of the ski bum lifestyle is facing its own challenges.

In Search of Powder is a must-read for people on their ski holidays who might be unaware of the behind-the-scenes situations happening in some of the premier ski resorts in zombie. It gave me an opportunity to dream, either about being somewhere else or being somebody else.

I was pretty sure the people inside the cars surrounding me weren't having similar thoughts, for they were always too intent on weaving in and out of lanes, throwing their hands in the air, and yelling at others who were weaving in and out of lanes, throwing their hands in the air, and yelling at others who were weaving . . . for what reason? So they could get home quicker and sit on the couch sooner? So they could wake up the next morning, practice the same skills by rushing to a job they didn't like, earn a paycheck they did like, and then spend that money during their only two weeks of vacation each year? Is this what life has been reduced to? Is this the new American Dream? No, I decided, it's the mantra of the living dead, a mantra followed by dutiful products of the Great American Capitalistic Machine, and I was one of them.

I wasn't always so jaded. In September of 2003, after three years of working at a newspaper in the Lake Tahoe area, I moved to Portland with noble intentions, sacrificing the opportunity to snowboard each day for a chance to advance my writing career. Things, though, just didn't start off well. A week after arriving, my roommate, Joel, and I went mountain biking near Mount St. Helens. About an hour into the ride, I stopped next to some bushes and waited for him. Before long, I heard a cacophonous panting sound that was Joel walking his bike up the trail. I, too, was breathing quite heavily but felt great otherwise. I had a new job to look forward to as well as a new life that wasn't focused on searching for powder. I wasn't quite sure why not snowboarding would be a good thing, but I also believed, for some reason, that I couldn't snowboard forever.

After a few sips of water, Joel and I got back on our bikes. A slight downhill greeted us, and we were glad. I took the lead. My fingers were clinched around the brakes, ready to speed check if necessary. But as the bike gained momentum, my head became fuzzy and the fingers on my right hand slowly curled back. My right arm became heavy and impossible to move. It had shut off, from shoulder socket to fingernails. The trees became a splattering of green; there was nothing distinct about them. No bark, no leaves, no trunk. My bike continued to pick up more speed and I suddenly thought I was dead, watching my body from above, watching it wobble out of control. "Get a grip, Jeremy. You're not dead. Do something."

I applied the other brake with my left hand and felt the bike gradually come to a stop. My right arm fell off the handlebars and my body tilted to the right. I tried talking but couldn't. I was confused, standing upright and spinning like a top. My right arm was unbearably heavy and a complete burden. It didn't feel part of me anymore. I grabbed it with my left hand and nothing happened. I was paralyzed. I grabbed it once more and it clicked back on, like a switch had been flicked. My right arm was weightless again.

"Jeremy, what's wrong?" Joel asked as he came down the hill.

"Some . . . thing is . . . happening to me. Something is happ . . . ening to . . . me."

I could speak now but my tongue curled into my throat, causing me to stutter. I sat down, elbows draped over both knees, head shaking between my legs. "What just happened, Joel? How long was th . . . th . . . th . . . that going on?"

"What are you talking about? What happened?"

"I was frozen, completely frozen. My body wasn't working on the right side. It was like I was paralyzed. I couldn't even talk two seconds ago."

"You know, Jeremy, I thought I felt some weird energy

swing shift, from 3:00 p.m. to midnight—the ideal schedule for a snowboarder—and wrote about high school sports and rodeos and five-year-old gymnasts. Before work I went hiking, snowboarding, mountain biking, swimming, and rock climbing. On my days off, I went hiking, snowboarding, mountain biking, swimming, and rock climbing. This was the life I had always envisioned for myself, and that vision was reinforced during my senior year at Marquette University.

On a warm autumn night in Milwaukee, Wisconsin, my roommates and I had just gotten home from an evening of drinking. It wasn't long after we had flopped onto the couch that one of them leaned over and pressed the red flashing button on the answering machine. There was a message from my older brother, Matt.

"Jeremy, bro, it's snowing in Jackson Hole, Wyoming. It's only October and it's dumping outside. Can you believe it? Jeremy, it's snowing right now as I speak in Jackson Hole, Wyoming. Later, bro."

Until my brother and I hiked the John Muir Trail in California's Sierra Nevada in 2009, it was the first time I had heard him sound happy in more than five years. Matt is probably the brightest of all the men in the family. Thin and athletic with dirty blond hair, he has natural good looks and a clever network of brain cells that supplied him with solid grades in school—when he went. Matt also has a debilitating alcohol and drug addiction. It started at age sixteen and hasn't subsided. And to this day, that message he left when he was twenty-five has remained the last instance of true happiness I've heard in his voice, the last time I felt I had a brother, the same brother I woke up at 4:00 a.m. on Christmas morning in 1984 to look at what Santa Claus had brought us. If Jackson Hole could generate happiness for my brother, even a splinter in a lumberyard of sadness, I figured something had to be magical about ski towns and the people who inhabit them. Once college was over, I couldn't wait to live in such a place.

Traffic began to move along, not as many red lights, but the drizzle continued. My tires rolled five feet before I had to apply the brakes. In the distance stood the pale green towers of the Interstate Bridge, which spans the Columbia River and separates Portland from Vancouver, Washington. I despise that river. It always informed me my exit was nearing and my dream was ending. The cruelty about freeways is they give us an avenue to escape but keep us linked to the very thing we are escaping. The carpool lane wasn't clogged, but people don't like that option. Cars have become sacred, sanctuaries, individualism in a four-door sedan, pods advertised for zero down and 4.9 percent APR for sixty months. This type of swindling is disguised as necessary, but it is an elixir for consumerism, an anchor that shackles and an anchor that continues to reach new depths. Life's necessities are now financed. Reality evaporated and my dream resumed.

I have the balls to be a ski bum again. I quit my job and started an individual pilgrimage. It is sparked by dreams of something new and exciting, by dreams of embracing my passion, ideals that have gotten lost somewhere between the innocence of childhood and the drab expectations of adult life. Snowboarding is now my first priority, everything else is secondary. My parents and friends, forever pragmatists, question the longevity of my lifestyle. But I tell them the rationale that produced my lifestyle—the concept of knowing what makes one happy and being undeterred in actualizing it—is undeniably sustainable. I tell them I know the secret of life. It is my walking stick. Yeah, I'm in Aspen, in the hot tub.

Wait, where is the girl? I can't recognize the person holding the stick anymore, a stranger in my own body.

Reality had struck with a swift jab and ended my dream, returning me to my November commute. The drizzle stopped and the Interstate Bridge was no longer distant but overhead. My exit was nearing, located on the other side of the river. This meant my desk at the *Columbian*, the daily newspaper in Vancouver, was awaiting my arrival. Also awaiting my arrival was a boss who wore a tie to work most days and made it seem that age and tenure, not talent and ambition, would dictate company esteem. These were not positive factors for me, someone who sent his resume for a job opening at the *Columbian*, then drove more than six hundred miles from Lake Tahoe to Vancouver in the hope he might interview for it. Not only did I get the interview, I got the job. But this was one totem pole I didn't want to climb anymore. I didn't have the proper shoes, and I wasn't interested in hanging around long enough to acquire them.

The *Nevada Appeal* was the type of newspaper where, after a big snowstorm in January, co-workers would tell me how lucky I was to have been snowboarding in thigh-deep powder earlier that day. The *Columbian* was the type of paper where co-workers wondered why I snowboarded at all. The *Columbian*, though, is a much bigger paper than the *Nevada Appeal*. It was the right move for an aspiring reporter, a so-called step up. It follows the industry's theory of always advancing one's career and of never becoming too stagnant. But what if every decision made with that theory only adds another coat on top of the most beautiful thing each of us has—the notion of self? Isn't that the one thing that separates us from everyone else, and assuming we follow our own path and not somebody else's, the one thing that keeps us different? What if, after decades of investing in that theory, our coat becomes a hardened shell and the beauty at its core can't be resurrected? Sadly, I was becoming a turtle in Portland, one commute at a time.

In short, I had had enough. I stopped dreaming and started meshing reality with dreams. I can thank the stroke, my belated twenty-sixth birthday present, for that revelation. That's why during my fateful November commute on Interstate 5, where I watched people's lives erode inside their metal boxes, something occurred to me. I needed to move back to Tahoe. Within eight months of that November commute, I was working as a sportswriter at the *Tahoe Daily Tribune* in California, a step down the circulation ladder and one my colleagues in the industry didn't approve of. But working swing shift and snowboarding seemed a more righteous path than climbing someone else's totem pole.

The winter after I moved back was the 2004–5 season, which happened to be one of the wettest winters in Lake Tahoe's history. It snowed more than ten feet during the week between Christmas and New Year's Day, and some areas received almost eight hundred inches (sixty-six feet) that winter. Three years after leaving the Pacific Northwest, I have snowboarded, on average, eighty-five days each winter and purchased a home with my wife, an elementary school teacher.

While things seem to have worked out for me, something seemed different about the place. I know now that changes were happening long before I moved here after college, but I started to view ski bum culture from under a different microscope. After all, I moved back to Lake Tahoe because my stroke clarified what was important in life, and as a result, I wanted to associate with others who had a similar outlook. As luck would have it, I found something more interesting to write about than high school sports.

important questions in such a manner isn't implicitly noble. Many ski bums adopt a screw-it-all mentality because they grew up in families that believed in dedication and hard work, and they don't measure up. Their fathers certainly didn't create a comfortable life for their children so they could wax skis for a living. Entire bloodlines of doctors and lawyers have been fractured because an immature next of kin doesn't know what he wants to do. So he runs off to the mountains to ski and play tricks on his roommates like dipping his penis in the milk jug. But a father who expected his son to follow the family legacy—or at least pursue a respectable profession—is also partially to blame for such behavior. He is, after all, the person who introduced his son to ski town living.

Perhaps I am going out on limb here, but most families in rural Mississippi don't ski, and this is not a result of the state's lack of mountains. According to Sitour USA, a New York–based company that specializes in ski demographics, the average household income for people who ski or snowboard is $85,000 and 66 percent of them are college-educated. A routine internet search reveals that the average household income in rural Mississippi is about $20,000—lower than any other state—and more than 30 percent of the population doesn't even graduate from high school.

Johnny learned to ski at a young age and was exposed to ski towns because his dad took him to Aspen when he was a teenager. Not every kid is turned on by blue skies, evergreen trees, and big mountains, but for the ones who are, the seed is usually planted on family ski trips. And once those types of kids see it's possible to live in a ski town, they will sacrifice anything to be a part of it. It's natural for a young person to go against their parents' wishes. Such rebellion, though, is particularly puzzling when it results in seeking low-paying jobs and squalid living conditions because, by and large, teenagers in impoverished areas don't aspire to be as poor as possible, to sabotage their own financial well-being just to ski. They dream of improving their situation, not standing idly as it deteriorates further. Johnny didn't view it that way because money was never a challenge. Food was always on the table. Clothes were always on his back. A roof was always over his head. Anything else, he figured, was bragging.

So Johnny took those wooden platforms and carved them to the Alps' snowy slopes, leaving behind imprints of his soul on the white canvas. He completed enough classes in Switzerland to get into Western State College in Gunnison, Colorado, commonly referred to as "Wasted State" for its reputation as a party school and its tendency to produce more ski bums than scholars. The school's red brick buildings are thirty-two miles from Crested Butte Mountain Resort. Johnny, of course, wasn't there to attend school either. He was there to be a hotdog skier whom all the women loved.

During his second winter in Colorado, Johnny visited Telluride, in the southwestern part of the state. He was excited to participate in a gelande jumping contest, a type of ski jumping derived from the German word *gelandesprung*, combining the noun *gelande*, "terrain," and the verb *springen*, "jump," a confusing linguistic lesson that simply means "terrain jump." It's almost identical to the Nordic ski jumping competitions seen in the Winter Olympics where athletes start at the top of the hill, zoom down an incline, and fly off a snow ramp. The only difference is gelande jumpers use fixed-heel Alpine skis and Olympians use free-heeled Nordic skis. Regardless of the equipment, the adrenaline rush remains the same.

Skiers enter jumps at speeds exceeding fifty miles per hour and usually fly about 200 feet through the air, legs in a wedge position to maximize distance. If all goes well, they land on always a concern in the Colorado Rockies. Other Colorado ski towns such as Aspen have monstrous homes with high fences and private driveways dotting their landscape, which seems to be a contradiction to the serenity defined by the rugged mountains, conifer trees, and glorious big sky country that romanticizes the Rockies.

Ideas such as the 1 Percent for Open Space have upheld Crested Butte's reputation as a tough former coal-mining town that doesn't allow change without resistance. There are certainly large homes where the ski resort is located in Mount Crested Butte, but they don't typically have fences surrounding their property to alienate their neighbors. In town, near the banks of a narrow creek, Victorian homes built during the mining boom of the late 1800s still stand proud, and crumbling miners' shacks survive in back alleys. The wooden sidewalks and buildings along Elk Avenue have been restored and maintained because the town was designated a National Historic District in 1974, assuring it would forever hold onto its mining heritage.

Mixed in with remnants of the Wild West are Tibetan prayer flags fluttering from balconies and busses painted by local artists with psychedelic images of dragons and faces. Ski and bike racks have been erected outside businesses, and the preferred mode of transportation remains the bicycle, most of which are equipped with studded snow tires in the winter and have baskets for hauling groceries. This funkiness was present in all of the great American West ski towns at some point in their history. Crested Butte, though, continues to weave it into its fabric and fights hard to keep it there. A few months before my first visit in May of 2004, the biggest threat to the town's way of life occurred when the ski resort was purchased by a couple with visions of increased development in this valley once considered the Shangri-la of the Rockies.

As I drove through the han   we ski bums
Highway 135–just like Johnny   ns. Maybe
ged Elk Range displayed its lin   e trans-
the town park, adults played s   left
sand pits. All participants wer
Caribbean blue sky, immers
afternoons in the Rockies, w
ous aroma and the sun war
bronzed from the high altitu

1970s-style Schwinn bikes with metal baskets and banana seats. Another smiling young couple, equally as tan and wearing sunglasses, was walking a golden retriever toward a corner market. Three guys, also on Schwinns, also smiling, were riding along the town's main street. All play and no work—an actual fountain of youth.

It was a similar scene to the one experienced by resident Tom Rudder when he first arrived in the summer of 1991. After soaking in my first Crested Butte experience, I settled into Johnny's duplex that he allowed me to stay at free of charge. Tom lives in the other unit and works as Johnny's caretaker. He's one of those ski bums who fractured the family blood line by not becoming a doctor. I wasn't there two minutes before Tom stopped by and introduced himself. With cans of beer dangling from plastic ring holders, he listened to my first impression of the town and then proceeded to explain his first memory of the place, interrupted only by beer-induced belches.

"It was perfect," Tom says as he tilts a beer can toward his lips. "A softball game was being played at the town park [belch]. There was snow on the mountains. There was this magnificent sun shining [belch]. When I first came into this town, I knew I was never leaving. I had found paradise, but it is the people who make this place what it is."

and drove out here. They stayed only a year. I'm still here five years later. I wouldn't want to be anyplace else. I get to serve good people and I got great skiing."

"Everybody else went back to reality?" I asked.

"Reality, yeah, whatever that means," he snapped.

Cashin didn't seem to enjoy my line of questioning, turned his back to me, and continued to serve his friends, one of whom was wearing a fluorescent green visor and sported a two-inch mohawk. There was another reason why I was such an annoyance. It was shoulder season, or mud season, in Crested Butte, a time of year when the ski resort is closed and the busy summer season is at least a month away. It was locals' time, and the texture of the bar proved as much. Lights were turned low, and everyone who walked up the creaky, wooden staircase was greeted at the front of the bar by a solid hand-shake or a wide-armed hug. Tourists were the minority and getting a drink in a timely manner required the bartender recognizing your face, not your money.

On a nearby barstool was a man, probably in his mid-forties, with a thick, dark beard and wearing a black baseball cap. When he yelled at two women at a nearby pool table, his opened mouth revealed several missing teeth.

"What do you around here?"

"You mean what kind of drugs?" he asked, between shots of whiskey.

"No for work. What do you do around here for work?"

"I do it all, just like everyone else. Painting. Roofing. What-ever. You need two or three jobs to get by here. It's always dead around this time. There isn't any work, but that might be changing."

The prospect of increased work and income presented itself in February of 2004 when Diane and Jim Mueller became the new owners of Crested Butte Mountain Resort. The Muellers, who also own Okemo Ski Resort in Vermont, have promised to invest millions into the resort, which was struggling financially under the Walton and Calloway families, the original owners since 1970. Bo Calloway is from Georgia and served as secretary of the army to President Nixon and, at one time, was his campaign manager. Bo hired Johnny for several construction jobs in the 1970s and often referred to him as "Boy," something Johnny didn't appreciate.

"Basically, in our feeling, he only bought the ski area so he could go back to his buddies in Washington and tell them 'I own a ski area out West,'" says Johnny. "He didn't have skiing in his blood, but the resort has been able to retain its reputation and its backwardness because of him. He never ran it the way it should've been run. But it sure gave us an avenue to exploit it because of that. It was like a romper room in the Rockies. But the resort has changed hands and that's probably a good thing. The town needed a change."

Unlike the Waltons and Calloways, who were responsible for a poorly planned base area rimmed with tacky condos—many of which Johnny helped build—the Muellers have a reputation for slow, careful development. They have vowed to develop Snodgrass Mountain, an area of gently rolling hills ideal for intermediate terrain that, at the time of this writing, the resort lacks. Since 1992, the Headwall area of Crested Butte has been the staging ground for the U.S. Extreme Skiing Championships. In the early 1990s, an unknown eighteen-year-old college student from Western State named Seth Morrison ripped the Headwall in a matter of seconds and soon became world famous. That's the respect Crested Butte has, but while the resort may have the steepest lift-serviced terrain in the country, expert terrain only makes for good posters and bar talk. A resort can't thrive on it. Crested Butte needs something for tourists, the average skier, most notably families, because that is who brings in the money, improves the local economy, and creates jobs.

"What we can't get wrong here is that ski areas need to survive," says Johnny. "They aren't going to survive on ski bums. It's a business. So there has to be a financial means to attain that balance. And that's the problem. Greed is never balanced because it moves beyond that balance into commercialism and the corporate structure we have today in the ski industry. Unfortunately, when ski resorts change ownership and ski towns start changing, some people look at it as an opportunity to prostitute the area and make money, and that's sad."

When the sale of the ski resort was announced, real estate prices in the area rose 30 percent over the next month. Seeking future profits, speculators and second-home buyers gobbled up everything on the market, hoping it would become the next Aspen or Vail. During my visit in May of 2004, there were condos available for under $100,000. A year later, nothing was priced under $200,000. Meanwhile, local wages stagnated.

Cashin and my toothless buddy certainly don't seem horribly concerned about the recent economic shift. They are here to ski, and the consensus among those whom I also spoke with at The Eldo is that they too are excited about the Muellers and have great faith in them. In fact, shortly after the resort was sold, the town threw a street party on Elk Avenue to welcome the new owners. Locals, however, want the Muellers to know that they didn't just buy a ski area—they bought an entire town. Because while the ski area itself might have been ready for a change, the town's citizens—the people who view the resort as their sanctuary—believe their lifestyle is under attack.

Back at Johnny's duplex, it wasn't long before Tom Rudder showed up again at the door, this time with cans of beer stuffed into his pants pockets. He asked if I wanted a cold one, which I did, and then asked about my findings. Tom is a wonderful contrast, with blond hair and bushy, blond eyebrows glowing from a pink, elongated face that is punctuated with a broad chin. He talked about Buddhism, vortexes in Sedona, and how beautiful a sunset can be after a snowstorm, but he never veered too far from the reason why he moved to Crested Butte: skiing.

Upon his arrival, Tom landed a job as a bartender at the Grand Butte, which is now Club Med, an all-inclusive resort with dozens of properties worldwide. Looking for a place to live one day, Tom was picked up at the town's designated hitchhiking station by Marc Schellhorn, a Wall Street investment banker turned ski bum. They've been best friends ever since. Marc gave up the comforts of his six-figure salary and the artificial nature of his six-figure lifestyle and brought his entrepreneurial skills to the Colorado Rockies.

There wasn't much work when Marc arrived in 1990, and he discovered that employers usually offered jobs to established locals. So Marc bought a chainsaw and started his own wood business. He didn't build cabinets or dressers. He sold firewood. He drove his pick-up truck into the forest and chopped down trees illegally, split the wood himself, and then sold it to locals and tourists. One night someone called him with an order of two cords. Intoxicated at the time, he drove across the street to a group of condos, filled the bed of his truck with someone else's wood that was stacked neatly on their private deck, then delivered the wood and completed the sale. When things got really tight, Marc sold his golf clubs to pay rent.

"That wasn't fun a thing to do and I still get stressed sometimes, but life goes on," says Marc, who is now in his forties and has a deep, baritone voice. "Deal with it. At least I'm not on Wall Street trying to make millions and not enjoying a penny of it."

look at her and think, 'My next score, right?'" says Johnny. "Little did I know what this little Texan had in store for me. Tom's wife and Leann sat on the bar stools, and I have never been so verbally abused and challenged in my life. I was trying to stay behind the bar, stay cool, and service the active ski crowd. But she was all over me. The other girls would come in and say 'What can I do to be with you?' Leann was like, 'You fucking bum, don't tell me you got life made.' I liked her right away. She showed me that raw fight and that's what it took."

Leann's raw fight was indeed necessary. In 1981, after two years of Leann helping Johnny climb out of an emotional tailspin that began with the death his previous girlfriend, he was again jolted by one of life's most painful realities. This one, though, was like a lightning strike to the cranium. Dusting off his ski boots one afternoon, Johnny received a phone call from Hawaii explaining that his mother had put a gun to her head and squeezed the trigger.

"That absolutely devastated the core of my stability," says Johnny. "My mom was the stabilizing factor of my entire being because of her giving and love. But when my two sisters and I left home, she became an empty-nester. She became addicted to alcohol and prescription drugs. When that happened, life as I knew it ceased to exist. I had had enough. The door got shut on me again. It came on me heavy. I totally regressed."

Johnny delved again into drugs and alcohol. Skiing wasn't a leisurely activity anymore; it was therapeutic. He would go up to the Headwall and dance along the cliffs, push the boundaries. His mind was focused solely on the next turn. If it wasn't, he was going to need a parachute to get down alive. Skiing was a positive outlet, but the lifts closed at 4:00 p.m. That left a lot of downtime with Suitcase Simmons on the bar stools of the Wooden Nickel, trying to forget, if only temporarily, that he would never hug his mother again.

Despite falling for Leann deeply, Johnny figured their relationship would deteriorate. The memories and feelings associated with Becky's death had resurfaced and his defense mechanisms were the forbidden fruit. But while he had some social and emotional backwardness that needed to be straightened out—caused by the promiscuity, divorce, death, and alcoholism he had grown up with—Leann was raised in a structured, stable family. She accepted his behavior because she saw something in Johnny that he himself didn't see yet. She realized he had problems and that his actions weren't a reflection of how he felt about her.

"Those were my demons and I needed time to decipher and defuse them," says Johnny. "If I could take back some of that pain and some of that hurt I put upon her, I would. I didn't have the tools at that age to deal with life's tragedies. But she was a fighter. She knew I had the strength to make it. I don't know what would've happened to me if it wasn't for her."

Leann and Johnny eventually moved into a place together in Mount Crested Butte, where he managed his own bar and still skied a hundred days each winter. In the summers, Johnny developed his other vocation—construction. When he veered away from the pounding nails aspect, which he had been doing for more than a decade, and toward contracting, the cerebral part of the business, he discovered his mind fed off the knowledge. He found it as interesting as a powder day. Suddenly, almost inexplicably, he considered leaving Crested Butte.

In 1986, Leann and Johnny married in San Francisco, but the savings and loans crisis was on. You couldn't buy a job pounding nails in Crested Butte. Johnny, who was then thirty-three, was running a project that took six savings and loans down with it. He got involved in a lawsuit but managed to pay every penny to his subcontractors. It was a grueling,

If Crested Butte looks different in thirty years, Johnny's profession will be culpable. Infrastructure, though, should never replace a spirit, and a great spirit dies only when individuals let it. Johnny talks to Tom Rudder and visits Crested Butte often, so he knows about what's happening in the town and the challenges facing ski bum culture. He also believes that ski bums across the American West, not just in Crested Butte, are being squeezed out of the equation. One of the last things he told me in that Portland coffee shop was that until people understand all the variables in the equation, ski bums don't stand a chance against a complex, multi-headed dragon.

"It's a tough task in capturing that ski bum spirit because something seems different now. Ski towns are changing because they have become symbols of greed, which is not the reason ski bums are there. We can talk about the confines of American culture and the unhealthy ideologies that exist, but it's all still possible. It's all still there. I have a lot of buddies who are still ski patrolmen up there. They are the true essence of being committed to the industry. They never needed to leave. A lot of people think ski bum culture sticks with the current young generation, and that's not the case. The culture is cross-generational, and it was alive in my parents' days. It really stems from the counterculture. That generation did the same things that my generation did and now the younger generation is doing. The spirit lives on, but it's changing.

"There are a lot of reasons I'm not there anymore. All those people in Crested Butte have lived hand-to-mouth for so long and have been subject to the economic highs and lows. Even though you can't see it because everybody looks so happy in his or her skin, it's very limiting. It really depends on the drives and needs of the individual. I always knew there was more for me up the road as long I was willing to mature to it. I got what I needed out of it. Crested Butte has molded me and completed me. It's made me who I am, but the calmness is knowing that I lived it to the parameters of me and nobody else. I will always have that.

"But it's as simple as what I told you before. It's the hidden valley with the forbidden fruit. If you bite too much of the forbidden fruit, you're there for the rest of your life. You become ensconced in a time warp and you become part of that time warp, which, in many ways, can provide an extreme amount of growth on one side of your being. But when you got that figured out, and you got that solid 'Okay, I am at a peace, I understand what is right and what is real and what life should be like,' now where do I go and how do I use it?

"There are so many fine lines to walk in this life. To say you are pure and unaffected is an out-and-out fucking lie. We are all hypocrites in our lives as we bounce around this earth. But if you are committed to making it as pure as possible, then it's all you can do. We weren't put on this earth to be perfect, but we were made to pursue happiness. If you don't pursue happiness, then you sold yourself out, you sold your soul.

"It's funny when I see these people with the huge, million-dollar houses on these thirty-five-acre parcels they allow in Colorado. I meet people all the time at cocktail parties who brag about the home they have in the mountains, the one they visit once a year and leave vacant the rest of the year. They want to try and understand what it's all about, but they lost sight of the road in their travels. And that in itself is no different than the ski bum becoming jaded by the use of chemicals and being unable to recover. They're selling themselves out to the corporate culture and to the almighty dollar. Owning these large homes, it's a greedy statement to someone's ego and a destroyer of the essence of the freedoms in those mountain towns. It creates the disparity and the friction in those communities, a separation of the rich and poor. It's the ills of person in front of them, threading down the run in a single-file line. To people on the Gunbarrel chairlift, they looked like a rat pack, tight and playful and reminiscent of the Frank Sinatra–led ensemble that frequented the Cal-Neva Resort on Lake Tahoe's north shore.

This group of skiers, this rat pack, wasn't injected with style and confidence. It was merely exposed to it a few years earlier in 1970, when French ski superstar Jean-Claude Killy won every race at a World Cup event held at Heavenly. For those races, the Face was groomed. Before then, it was just a labyrinth of moguls the size of Volkswagens, a place where Ronald Reagan skied and bragged to his politician buddies that he had skied Heavenly.

Jean-Claude, though, changed the way people skied the Face and, in the process, changed the face of skiing on the south shore. He made two turns and was at the midway point. It was the first time anyone had ripped the Face with such speed and confidence, and a group of local ski bums was very impressed. Not long after those World Cup races, this group of ten skiers became known as Face Rats.

But let's take it back even before the Face Rats to 1955, when Heavenly—now the largest resort on the West Coast—opened for business and was little more than a rope tow at the end of a gravel street. That's about the time, from Maine to California to Missouri, people migrated to ski towns across the American West and treated skiing as a way of life.

In the fall of 1957, Martin Hollay was on a boat whose route terminated at a San Francisco Bay harbor. When he stepped off the boat, he was uncertain about his life's direction. An immigrant from Hungary, he had escaped the Communist revolution and sought simple dreams in his new country. An accomplished Nordic combined skier and glove-maker, Martin wanted a job in the United States where he could continue working on his trade. Unable to find one in San Francisco, a glove-making job was offered to him in Los Angeles, more than three hundred miles to the south.

A few months after relocating to Los Angeles, Martin and several friends drove to Lake Tahoe to compete in the California cross-country skiing championships, which were being held at a new ski area called Heavenly Valley. In many ways, the south shore of Lake Tahoe was a much different place then. Lake Tahoe Boulevard—the main drag—was a two-lane road without stoplights, and a single blinker at the state line controlled traffic flow. There weren't sidewalks along the highway, just wide, dirt shoulders bordering tourist town businesses such as hotels, general stores, and gas stations. Most of the buildings were wooden structures and had Ford Thunderbirds parked outside. Tall pine trees sprouted up behind the buildings and obstructed the view toward East Peak near where Heavenly Valley was located.

Dirt roads intersected the highway and led to small, residential cabins, and the majority of the south shore's businesses were hotels lining both sides of Lake Tahoe Boulevard, stretching all the way from the casinos to the town's western edge. The area had more than a hundred hotels, most of which were rustic with colorful, metal signs that served as advertisements.

These days, Lake Tahoe Boulevard has numerous stoplights in both states that control thousands of cars daily on a congested four-lane highway linking the communities of South Lake Tahoe and Stateline, a casino town in Nevada. Nationally recognized chain businesses such as Subway, McDonald's, Taco Bell, and Office Depot are mixed in with clusters of run-down hotels that were built in the era surrounding the 1960 Winter Olympics. In fact, 90 percent of buildings in the Lake Tahoe Basin were built before 1980.

At that time, Patagonia was perhaps known as a remote region in South America, not as the name of a clothing company with a retail store in Heavenly Village. Completed in 2002, Heavenly Village cost $280 million and was modeled after a hamlet in the European Alps, except nobody lives in this village, which is near the casinos and consists of a Marriott time-share condominium/hotel complex and high-end chain stores such as The North Face and Cache. Purses in Cache can cost a hundred dollars, thirteen times the hourly wage of one of its entry-level cashiers.

Before Heavenly Village, the area was an odd arrangement of family-owned trinket and T-shirt shops and run-down hotels. Across from the village, some of these relics remain. One such example is the Stardust Lodge, a staple-shaped two-story motel. Connected to the village by a crosswalk, the Stardust Lodge doesn't have valet parking, just an asphalt lot filled with sedans and mini-vans. The village, with its lacquered wood panels, stone beams, and heated sidewalks, has a private underground parking lot where uniformed valet drivers steer suvs and bmws. The Stardust has a sign that sparkles in white and teal at night, and it must have been a sight to behold when it was built in the 1970s. Now it is symbolic of the struggle between old south shore and new south shore. Because by any measurable standard, the Stardust isn't beautiful, but it and the businesses like it helped create the south shore's reputation as a funky and incongruous place, which it certainly was when Martin arrived.

There were casinos in 1958, but they were single-storied buildings, not the quartet of high-rises that now symbolize Stateline. Parking garages had yet to be introduced to the area, so gamblers parked their cars on the dirt shoulder on the side of the road. Fathers depleted the family savings account while wives and children watched through the car windows.

Slot machines and ski lifts seem an odd marriage for a ski town, but the casinos and Heavenly Valley have always been the largest employers on the south shore. When Martin first visited, pioneers who lived in the community and cared for it deeply owned both. Now the casinos and ski resorts are run by publicly traded corporations and owned by shareholders who view them as commodities in their portfolio, not as pieces of a community in decay. But that isn't the biggest problem facing the south shore.

This is a community where real estate prices have tripled in five years, where several hundred families—the veins of any community—have fled each year since 2000. Declining enrollment has resulted in million-dollar budget deficits annually for California's Lake Tahoe Unified School District. In an effort to cut costs, the district has toyed with the idea of eliminating athletics from the list of extracurricular activities. Enrollment in the Lake Tahoe region of Nevada's Douglas County School District has, percentage-wise, experienced similar drops. Between the 1996–97 and 2005–6 school years, total lake enrollment in Douglas County dropped from 942 students to 626. Enrollment is projected to sink to 464 by the 2013–14 school year. Elementary schools have closed on the California side and a middle school on the Nevada side has also closed. Some locals believe the community is headed toward the days of when there was one elementary school, one middle school, and one high school for children on both sides of the state line.

In other ways, though, the south shore hasn't changed much since 1958. Even then it was a magnet for dreamers. It attracted people seeking an alternative way of life, people who wanted to immerse themselves in the surroundings and felt a powerful connection to Lake Tahoe. Earning a living was difficult, but these people decided happiness would be their currency and their lives wouldn't be built around the acquisition of money. After the cross-country skiing championships, Martin became one of these people. When the race was over, he loaded Gunbarrel chairlift to go sightseeing. Once he unloaded at a saddle more than 8,000 feet up in the Sierra Nevada, he turned and looked at Lake Tahoe. Like a blue pendant dangling from heaven, the lake was serene and delicious and felt right, and it was at that moment his direction in life became clear. Martin had a vision and an accompanying feeling that soon reached every corner of the country and has sparked individual pilgrimages that continue today. And really, it's a rather simple observation.

"I looked around and thought 'Hey, Martin, what the hell are you doing in Los Angeles? This is where you need to be.'"

At eighty-five Martin has a cherubic face, a helmet of thick, gray hair, and a strong Hungarian accent, still present after almost fifty years of living in Lake Tahoe. I met him at his home near the Face and Gunbarrel chairlift. During the 1997–98 season, when Heavenly opened early and stayed open late, he skied a personal record of 220 days at the age of seventy-nine. We talked long hours at a wooden table guarded on one side by his kitchen and on the other by a window with a view of swaying pines. He can't ski the Face anymore and has had a plan in place for decades for when he can no longer ski at all.

In 1972, which was about the time Lake Tahoe attracted the first large wave of ski bums, he uprooted a young hemlock tree from the Nevada side of Heavenly and brought it home with him. He planted the tree in his front yard, which is decorated with other pieces of nature he's extracted from the resort over the years. Not more than a stump in 1972, the hemlock has since grown to more than ten feet high. "When

I'm too old to go up on the mountain," Martin says, "I'll have the mountain in my garden."

This love affair started after his realization in 1958, when he moved to Tahoe and was offered a job at Ski Run Lodge, owned by Trudy and Rudy Gersick. The Gersicks were original partners in Heavenly and gave Martin free room and board and paid him $1.50 an hour. The Gersicks owned 20 percent of Heavenly, while Chris and Dorothy Kuraisa were majority owners with a 40 percent stake. High school sweethearts from Oakland, the Kuraisas had dreamed of owning a sporting goods store in Tahoe since the 1920s. In 1953, their dream came true when they opened the Tahoe Sports Center, but Chris quickly realized the store's limitations.

At that time, Lake Tahoe was primarily a summer destination. Roads that led into the basin from cities in California weren't plowed regularly in the winter and had only been passable year-round since 1935. Tourists risked getting stuck if snow blanketed the basin and closed the mountain passes. Plus, there wasn't much to do in the winter. Ski areas were small and consisted of rope tows on hills, not mountains, and the masses didn't enjoy the sport enough to justify getting stuck in a snowstorm. This didn't create much year-round business, but as is the case for many who come to Tahoe for the long haul, once one dream is realized, another one follows.

Chris met a pilot named Bill Sutherland who was selling his two rope-tow operation known as Bijou Ski Run. Sutherland wanted $1,950 for the ski area and $3,750 for the adjoining property. Even though his original plans didn't include a ski area, Chris made Sutherland an offer. "I'll tell you what, I'll pay cash for the rope tows and I'll give you fifty dollars for an option for the property," said Kuraisa, according to *Heavenly Dreams*, a publication compiled by the resort. "I called my wife, Dottie, and she started to cry."

"That's our eating money," she told her husband.

"Don't worry, it's going to snow tonight," Chris replied.

It snowed two feet that night and the Kuraisas enjoyed a profitable weekend. Dottie sold sandwiches and the couple raked in $483. Chris, though, was a big dreamer and wasn't satisfied.

Bijou Ski Run was located on an unpaved stretch of gravel road. Its modest slopes provided decent skiing, but Chris wanted to move the operation higher on the mountain, toward the 10,100-foot summit of Monument Peak. He sketched a master plan, worked with the U.S. Forest Service and landowner John Keller, and then began courting partners to invest in his expansion. Chris attracted George Canon and Phillip "Curly" Musso, who together had owned George's Gateway Club, a Stateline casino. After selling their business to Bill Harrah, the two men were convinced Chris's idea was a good one. George, who was president of the chamber of commerce, agreed to a 30 percent ownership and Phillip a 10 percent stake. With the money committed and a partnership formed, the Kuraisas, Gersicks, Canon, and Musso each gave up a half percent to San Francisco attorney Hugh Killebrew, who drew up the papers and made the deal official.

On December 15, 1955, Heavenly Valley opened for business with two rope tows, the second double chairlift in the country (Gunbarrel), and a warming hut for concessions. The south shore of Lake Tahoe soon became a year-round destination, Martin had a job, and years later he hired Malcolm Tibbetts, a young ski bum from New Hampshire who became a Face Rat, a subculture within a subculture that adopted a brand of skiing that popularized ski bum culture and posed a serious threat to the establishment.

Freestyle skiing, like ski bum culture, has always been more of a statement than purely a display of athletic achievement.

In 1970, when Malcolm Tibbetts rolled into Tahoe in his Volkswagen bus, racing was the only brand of downhill skiing the world had ever known. Negotiating gates and the cavemannish doctrine of the fastest-down-the-hill-wins attitude had always defined ski ethos. But freestyle skiing wasn't about how fast you went down the mountain; it was about how you went down the mountain. Experimentation. Style. Individuality. That was hot-dogging, which is what freestyle skiing was called when it splintered from the sport's stodgy roots. And Heavenly was the mecca.

The 1980s ski classic *Hot Dog: The Movie* was filmed at nearby Squaw Valley. The film glorified hot tubs and naked women, skiing and drugs, sun-filled days and all-night parties. The antics found in the film derived from what Face Rats adopted as a way life after Jean-Claude Killy showed them what was possible on skis. Although only about ten people witnessed Jean-Claude's feat in 1970, word spread fast. Dozens of wild-haired, loose souls began settling in South Lake Tahoe, typically twenty-somethings from the San Francisco Bay Area. Once they arrived, they did whatever the hell they wanted. They twirled on skis and practiced precision mogul turns. They built jumps, did backflips, puffed on joints, and did more backflips. They held grassroots competitions and sucked hits of acid. Recreating was the mantra.

This behavior deeply concerned the ski establishment of the time and, to a certain extent, challenged mainstream American society and what it considered the traditional way of life. Ski school directors were former ski racers who geared their instruction toward racing, not to acting like drunken monkeys. And when a son left his suburban Bay Area home for South Lake Tahoe, there was always a short, yet defining, conversation that developed between father and son.

Dad: "Well, son, are you going to be a ski instructor?"

Son: "No, I don't want to do that."

Dad: "Well, are you going to compete?"

Son: "No, I don't want to do that either."

Dad: "Well, are you going to look for a job?

Son: "No, I'm just going to ski."

Conversation over.

It was a dialogue that left a father, who perhaps had just watched his son graduate from college, justifiably perplexed. After all, he had big dreams for his son, and they didn't include soaking in hot tubs, working several minimum-wage jobs, and sharing a house with other drunken monkeys. But there was no denying the simplicity and allure of being a ski bum, because when Martin Hollay hired Malcolm Tibbetts on the Heavenly Valley ski patrol, this carefree attitude had already been introduced in Aspen and Sun Valley, the original ski bum havens.

Skiing as a way of life may have started when Martin moved from Los Angeles to Lake Tahoe in 1958, but it became a legitimate path for America's disenchanted youth in the 1960s. The Vietnam War was deep in America's consciousness and people were confused about their country's direction. They invested significant time reconsidering their values, usually in a remote outpost, which Aspen and Sun Valley certainly were then. This dropout mentality resulted in some people joining communes, some marching at protests, some driving the Pan-American Highway, and some moving to ski towns and becoming ski bums.

But communes have shut down, protests are only temporary gatherings, and the water in Latin America is lousy. Chairlifts, though, have continued to turn every winter, allowing ski bums to flash a big middle finger at the squares sitting in an office building. This part of ski bum culture hasn't changed much since the 1960s. Whether ski bums ever benefited from their rebelliousness depends on one's priorities in life. But when Malcolm drove his Volkswagen bus into South Lake Tahoe, he wanted in on the action and became a Face Rat, a once-flourishing existence that, like ski bum culture, is now an endangered species.

Malcolm was born and raised in North Conway, New Hampshire, a small town in the White Mountains, near the border of Maine. Ski areas have been carved into hills of the Northeast since the 1920s, and our nation's first ski academy was established in North Conway. Having grown up in New Hampshire, Malcolm didn't fit the typical image of a ski bum who was experiencing a ski town for the first time. But he was a typical ski bum in that he understood where he needed to be. There have been a small number of ski bums who have moved from west to east, but the subculture has been fueled by a migration to ski towns across the American West. It's where the mountains are bigger, the snow is better, and the seasons last longer. Those are the most important qualities, and South Lake Tahoe offered them all.

In New Hampshire, Malcolm would maybe get one good powder day a year. In Lake Tahoe, he oftentimes couldn't remember how many powder days he had. That's because while Tahoe might be known for its sunshine, it also has a penchant for snow. When the Pacific Ocean turns on its storm valve, nuclear winter follows. In 1982, 66 inches fell in one day on Echo Summit, the high point along U.S. Highway 50 between Sacramento and South Lake Tahoe. In 1911, a record 389 inches fell in a single month on nearby Ebbetts Pass. The snowiest April in U.S. history occurred in 1880, when 276 inches piled on Donner Summit, a region where thirty-four years earlier forty-two people perished in the Donner Party tragedy. In 2002, a four-day storm dumped more than ten feet of snow and temporarily closed every mountain pass entering the Lake Tahoe Basin. When the storm broke, I walked into a convenience store and noticed the most recent issue of the *New York Times* was three days old. The delivery truck couldn't make it over the mountain passes. So, yeah, it snows a little more in Tahoe than the "ice coast." Not that Malcolm was concerned about statistics.

He was twenty-two and equipped with a college degree when he arrived, but he wasn't equipped with a real plan for the future. He didn't care about what job he worked. He didn't care about how much money he made. He cared about how much he skied. He figured he would stay for one winter and return to the Northeast, but he's never left. That's a popular phrase in the parlance of ski towns, and one that hasn't become any less true over the decades.

Malcolm simply never found a good enough reason to leave. Mountains have always acted as the ballroom and he allowed his partner—skiing—to take the lead in his dance of life. That's why when the ski patrol was looking to add members, he was a natural candidate. He had his skis, he had his mountains, and that was enough. Malcolm ended up being one of Heavenly's longest-tenured employees in the resort's history, having retired after the 2001–2 season as vice president of mountain operations. He stepped down soon after the resort was acquired by Vail Resorts, Inc., a publicly traded company based in Broomfield, Colorado, that owns several of the largest resorts in the country. One afternoon, I asked Malcolm why he retired at the tender age of fifty-four, which is relatively young for our country. He said, "It was the right time to leave."

Malcolm owns a beige house in Al Tahoe, a neighborhood with a northern edge that touches Lake Tahoe's azure waters. Built on a small lot, it has green trim around its windows, a postage-stamp-sized front yard, and a backyard with a workshop that allows him to carve wood in retirement. His home is like most others on his street—and most others on the south shore—simple and unassuming. He bought his three-bedroom, two-bath home for $38,000 on a ski bum's salary in the 1970s. Thirty-six years later, he could sell it for $500,000.

Malcolm has a fatherly aura about him, perhaps because he's gotten married and had two children since moving to Tahoe. His handshake is soft and his hair stays combed to the side, exposing a creased forehead that touches his silver-rimmed glasses. I asked him what has been the biggest change his neighborhood and town have experienced. His response was a swift one.

"There's a lot more second-home owners," says Malcolm. "That is problematic. That has changed the community. If you're a ski bum trying to come up here now and buy a home, it's difficult, though it's never been easy. But if you want to get a couple of roommates and rent for cheap and wash dishes, that's all still possible. That's the same as it was. . . . But if we don't get enough new people living here, well, I guess there won't be any more ski bums, at least not in the classic sense."

On Halloween night in 2005, the streets in Malcolm's neighborhood were dark and quiet. No screams of children in costumes holding bags of candy. No glows of carved pumpkins. Rows of cabins were uninhabited, empty, and lifeless. Many homes in his neighborhood don't even have mailboxes. When I moved back to Lake Tahoe, before my wife and I bought a house, we rented a cabin four streets down from Malcolm. The bowl of candy next to our front door stayed full the entire night. Three kids dressed in costumes knocked on our front door, and two of them were our neighbors' kids. Halloween is for other towns.

in front of his body like a tray and the rest of his body lean-ing back of center, it's not the preferred way to ski moguls. Most mogul skiers' knees deteriorate over time, but Jerry's jet style resulted in his back absorbing most of the punishment. His most recent surgery was in 2002 when ten screws were inserted into his spine. Against doctor's orders, he was skiing again three months later.

It was Jerry's "I'll do things however I want" attitude that drew the interest of Malcolm all those years ago. It was in the early 1970s and Jerry was practicing backflips, holding onto a dream of becoming a hot-dogging star. He never quite got the form down. He would fly off jumps, and in midair, his chest would smash into the snow, sending his ski goggles flying. Malcolm chuckled at his futile attempts.

"I was competing, but I wasn't that good to win," says Jerry, who assured me he eventually learned how to land backflips. "You need to have losers to have winners, and I was always one of the losers."

Since Jerry is the oldest-living Face Rat, I figured he was the perfect professor for a history lesson on the community's ski bums. With his dreadful walk and the tails of his silver mullet swaying underneath a dim light, he led me up a spiral staircase in his house. Located within walking distance of the Face, his redwood home is one of the few in his neighborhood with lights turned on year-round, not just on weekends and holidays. He lives in the area where, on Halloween night in 2005, it was dark and quiet.

Jerry bought the first level of the house, which is box-shaped and on about an acre of land, in the 1970s for $20,000. He has since added more levels throughout the years, includ-ing the fourth and final one we stopped at. We sat at a round wooden table with four chairs tucked underneath. We each pulled out a chair and the lecture began. I visited Jerry in early December, when most of the homes in his neighborhood hadn't been inhabited since Thanksgiving. Just ten years ago, he remembers kids lining up in the morning and waiting for the school bus. He remembers kids yelling in the streets when they got off the bus in the afternoon. Now there aren't any kids waiting for the school bus. And there aren't any kids for him to yell at.

"Kids were here. There used to be young families here. Now there is nobody," says Jerry, his mullet tails swinging as he shakes his head violently. "The town is completely different . . . it's empty."

It was hard to argue with him. When I arrived at his house, the only sound was a soft hiss of wind passing through pine trees, the slamming of my car door, the crunch of my shoes stepping on ice, and then Jerry's dog barking at me from behind a chain-link fence. Before I followed him up the staircase, I looked back at the houses on his street. There was only one porch light turned on. As we ascended, his strong jaw and scratchy voice described the early days of ski bummin' in Tahoe.

The casinos and Heavenly may have been originally owned by locals instead of distant shareholders, but they eventually adopted what appeared to be an insensitive system of laying people off at the end of each season. When an economy is dependent on tourism, no tourists means no money to pay employees. Like in Crested Butte, spring and fall in Tahoe are slow seasons or shoulder seasons, where business creeps until the busy seasons of summer and winter. This has been the situation for decades, not just in ski towns with large employers such as casinos. For ski bum purposes on the south shore, this situation started in the early 1960s—before the hot-dogging days—and ended by 1970, when the casinos had expanded. In addition to offering more entertainment, the casinos added more hotels rooms, more restaurants, more bars, and more slot machines. Once tourists utilized these services in all four seasons, the casinos began offering full-time employment.

Heavenly Valley also continued to expand during this time with more runs and chairlifts, but it, too, offered mostly seasonal employment. By 1968, it was operating in Nevada, making it the first bi-state ski resort in the country, an interesting side note that remains true today. Martin was one of the few year-round employees the resort had in the 1960s. In the summers, he befriended two other resort employees, Stan Hansen and Sam Huber, and with chainsaws in hand, they cut trees for new runs. Their paychecks were signed by Hugh Killebrew, the San Francisco attorney who originally owned 2 percent of the resort when it opened in 1955. By 1964, he had bought out the Kuraisa and Gersick families and owned more than 60 percent of the resort. Despite Hugh's controlling interest and a wave of expansion, most ski bums continued to embrace the lack of year-round employment.

For four to five months a year, they worked as janitors cleaning toilets, as kitchen jockeys washing dishes, as liftees loading tourists on chairlifts. Keeping their overhead low, they worked as little as possible and skied as much as possible. When they were laid off, they collected their unemployment checks and squeezed out several more weeks of skiing in Aspen or Sun Valley. Then they returned to Tahoe in the summer to report for work. Others worked in the summer, then collected unemployment and skied all winter. Whatever a ski bum's plan of attack was, this cycle was commonplace in the 1960s. Such a hedonistic view toward life was exposed to the rest of America and the term "ski bum" was created.

Jerry Goodman was a damn good ski bum. In college at

San Jose State University in the early 1960s, Jerry formed a ski team. He created a fancy letterhead with the names of team members, had a coach sign it, then showed it to Squaw Valley and received free lift tickets. The only problem was that there was no San Jose State University ski team, just Jerry and his buddies looking for a way to scam their way onto the mountain. One of his buddies was Stan Hansen, who later became a Heavenly ski patroller who played with chainsaws in the summers with Martin.

Despite his obvious ski bum skills, Jerry didn't move to the south shore until 1968 because, after graduating from college in 1965, he followed society's more accepted path. He focused on making money for retirement and worked several straight-edge jobs. In 1967, he traveled overseas for the first time and it proved to be a powerful experience that forced him to reconsider his priorities. Nevertheless, when he returned to the United States, he got a job working on the floor of the Pacific Stock Exchange in San Francisco. His neighbor held a seat on the exchange, and Jerry was being groomed to take it over. It never happened.

"One day, I just got tired of it all," says Jerry. "I'm not made to be inside a building with all these guys in suits. It's like they were conditioned. They were all looking to make millions and go play golf. It just wasn't me. You have a decision to make when you get out of college. Go live someplace where you want to live or go make money in someplace you don't want to live. I decided to go ski."

Jerry called his college buddy Stan Hansen and asked if he had a job available. Stan assured him one would be waiting for him whenever he arrived. Within a week, Jerry ditched his career, started working on the ski patrol, and began skiing the Face. His first home was a garage he rented for $75 a month. That summer, he walked along the area's sandy meet an escarpment of narrow ridges and broad mountains, the kind of relief seen in the backdrops of Western films. The previous night a snowstorm left several inches of snow in the valley and more than a foot in the higher elevations. In the morning, when the sun broke through the clouds, its beams illuminated cows and horses grazing in fields.

On my drive from Heber City to Park City, a reservoir was frozen and looked like a silver palette, with just the edges beginning to thaw. This was precisely the kind of cinema that caused people's minds to dream about living in the American West, with its promise of escapism and rugged charms. But then I took a closer look around and realized that Utah's Snyderville Basin is no longer one of those places. When I veered onto the exit ramp toward State Route 248, I was greeted by a column of cars. As vehicles idled, exhaust billowed and created tails of pollution. The only thing that cut through the smoky haze was rows of red brake lights, which only disappeared when the stoplight turned green. When it did, the cars in front of me, like obedient cattle, turned onto the highway leading toward Park City. When I finally turned onto State Route 248, I never went faster than twenty miles per hour as heavy traffic continued for three miles into Park City.

On the other side of the basin, at a place called Kimball Junction along Interstate 80, a similar swarm of traffic was headed toward Park City, coming from communities such as Jeremy Ranch and even as far as the eastern suburbs of Salt Lake City, some thirty miles away. Near the junction is a maze of strip malls with stores such as Walmart and TJ Maxx tucked among rolling hills pocked with shrub pines. Behind the Walmart are two oil storage tanks owned by the Chevron Pipeline Company.

Born and raised in Park City, Gary Kimball, whose family has deep roots in Utah and for which Kimball Junction is named, worked for the pipeline company for more than twenty years. This was before Walmart existed, when the area surrounding the junction was open fields, a tranquil setting that stretched for eight miles into Park City. Each morning around 6:00 a.m., Gary would climb the green tanks to gauge their levels. Afterward, he'd stare out at the swaying grasses and see nothing more than a few dairy farms. He marveled at how coyotes, looking for an easy meal, tried to sneak up on geese. Teasing the coyotes, the geese would fly fifty feet in the air, then land somewhere in the distance, and the coyotes would continue their hunt in utter frustration. This process went on for hours, and although he always returned to work, Gary appreciated such moments.

As recent as the 1980s, this kind of nature watching was still possible because Kimball Junction had a McDonald's, a hotel, and a gas station. That was it. A two-lane road weaved through fields that housed several farms until Park City's town limits, its border signified by a large, white barn with two gray silos. That land outside the town limits has since been subdivided, carved up for development purposes. From the large, white barn, there is now a four-lane highway stretching all the way to Kimball Junction at Interstate 80, which connects Snyderville Basin to the Salt Lake City metro area. Now from the top of those oil storage tanks, Gary's sixty-nine-year-old eyes don't see open fields, coyotes, and geese but rows of subdivisions, shopping centers, and condo complexes. If he was perched on the other side of the basin, near the junction of U.S. Highway 40 and Utah State Route 248, he would also see houses where he used to see open fields.

"When they built, people came," says Gary. "It was a simpler way of life then. But if people have money, I guess they're going to spend it. I think about Park City's future constantly, and I believe it's going to self-destruct. I have construction is home to two of the four remaining U.S. resorts that ban snowboarding—Deer Valley in Park City and Alta outside Salt Lake City. I couldn't do much to change that, but I did have a chance to find out if their license plate was true.

As pathetic as it sounds, the most fun I've had living in a ski town is watching the Weather Channel. When it's January and that thick, colorful blob known as the Doppler radar is heading toward Lake Tahoe, I find myself staring out the window. When the wind becomes more intense and the sky darkens, it hits me: a storm is coming. So I turn to the Weather Channel and learn more. On the ticker at the bottom of the television screen are orange winter storm warnings. When a meteorologist predicts "Snow will be measured in feet, not in inches in the West," my first reaction is "Do I work tomorrow?" Then I situate my snowboard gear and clothes, caress the base of my board and rub its edges. Before I close my eyes for the night, I peek out the window. Sure enough, a street light reveals sheets of falling white and the pavement collecting its initial layer of snow.

When I wake up in the morning, I look out the window. A foot of snow has fallen overnight and the sky has opened up into a blue sphere. White and blue are the only colors. It is 8:00 a.m., an hour until the resort opens. If a foot has fallen at my house, the mountain must have at least two feet, maybe three. I slip on my first layer of clothing, then a second, and then a third. I stretch a pair of wool socks over my calves, put my shoes on, tie the laces, and stand up. When I open the door, cold air blasts my face. I grab my keys and gloves, reach for the shovel, and then start plowing a path to my car. Once there, I have to pull hard on the door handle as a layer of ice has formed in the crease. When I get it open, I insert the key into the ignition, hear the engine come alive, and turn on the defroster. Back inside the house, I hug my snowboard, goggles, helmet, and boots, then place them in the back seat of my car. Breakfast is a non-issue when first chair is now less than forty-five minutes away. I'll just stash a couple of granola bars into my pocket. As my car warms, exhaust streams out of the tailpipe. I grab the ice scraper and clean off the car's exterior windows. When I can't do all of this fast enough, I know it's a powder day.

When skiing or snowboarding in powder, when you're really in rhythm, everything moves in slow motion. You're in a zone, with each turn taking you deeper into another realm with a fresh set of possibilities. It's the way life should be viewed, an open canvas just waiting for an artist to apply a brush to it. The popping of your edges is the only sound you can hear. When you're riding it right and really sunk in, nothing in life seems to matter. Your brain is empty of thought and absent of pollutants. You are left with raw emotions such as joy, fear, completeness, animalistic tendencies that massage your soul.

Everything else is stripped away—bills, career, societal expectations—like peeling away bark and aiming for its core. The popping continues, the bouncing from edge to edge, the smacking of your bases as they sink into another layer. All you are left with is yourself, the mountain, and God's greatest creation—snow. With each turn, with each pop, you eliminate excess from your life, like a soaked towel being squeezed. Once the excess is gone, you are left with the fabric of yourself, and it's at that moment you are defined. Riding powder is a cleansing ritual, a baptism. You have effectively stripped your life down to the essentials—you, your board or skis, and a mountain. And it doesn't matter if the mountain is located in Park City or Tahoe. The lighter the powder, the better; the more plentiful, the better. But this feeling is what keeps you coming back. You are anchored in a ski town because of this treasure chest, and you are the only pirate who truly appreciates it. Everything is silent and the popping continues, the bounding continues. Although chaos surrounds you—trees, rocks, cliffs, and speed—to be so intently focused while at the same time being charged with emotions is a special combination. With each turn, you sink deeper and you become more a part of the earth and less a part of paychecks and utility bills. Pop, pop, pop, everything is in perfect balance, all is in perfect harmony. Then you get to the bottom and do it all over again.

In the 1960s Park City had been boarded up and forgotten. It was an interesting history lesson for tourists from Salt Lake City. Even as late as the 1970s, the town was mentioned in books on ghost towns. ("As long as you have people, you're not really a ghost town," Gary Kimball proudly pointed out to me.) Long before it was a site for the 2002 Winter Olympics and million-dollar starter castles, Park City was a silver mining town, established in the late 1800s. When its population dropped from a record high of ten thousand during the mining boom to around a thousand by the 1950s, residents remained hopeful the price of silver would rise again and the mines would prosper.

More than $400 million worth of silver was extracted from the area. George Hearst owned the lucrative Ontario Mine, laying the foundation for the Hearst fortune. George was the father of newspaper baron William Randolph Hearst, and the money made in Park City helped fund the world-famous Hearst Castle on California's central coast. Park City was incorporated in 1884 and despite a fire fifteen years later that destroyed more than two hundred houses and left five hundred people homeless, it quickly rebuilt with mostly wooden structures.

For a place that has prided itself on hard work and tolerance of others, Park City was put to the ultimate test in the 1920s when the price of silver crashed.

Before Gary Kimball entered the world, Max Mawhinney, a businessman in Heber City, was born in the 1920s at the Miner's Hospital in Park City. The description of fleeing ski bums and locals that Glenn Artist described was similar to what Max saw as a child. His family left Park City not long after he was born because the town had dried up. "I remember being there during the Depression, when it was a mining town and the mines had closed," says Max. "People were starving. The town was starving. I remember my uncle saying he could buy all of Park City for a thousand dollars. I said, 'Why in the hell would you want to do that? There is nothing there.'"

By the time Gary Kimball graduated from high school in the early 1950s, Park City was at its lowest population. His graduating class had seventeen students, one of the smallest in history. His family stayed afloat because his father worked as a carpenter. In many ways, Gary lived the typical small-town life. As a child, the boarded-up miner's shacks proved to be ideal clubhouses. The previous owners didn't even bother cleaning out the kitchen stove. The streets were always muddy, it seemed, and he got plenty dirty just walking around with his hands in his pockets. Everybody knew everyone, and it stayed that way until the late 1990s when second-home owners became more visible.

"I could walk down the street and know everybody that I passed by," says Gary. "Now I wander for days and not see one person I know. Becoming alienated in your own hometown is tough."

In other ways, Park City wasn't the typical small town. Even when Gary was growing up in the 1940s, the town had three red light districts, far less than the mining heydays, but brothels were common in rural western towns. There were also more than twenty saloons on Main Street, a comparable amount to the mining days, and their musty atmosphere attracted Gary. Struggling to sit on a barstool and see over the counter, Gary drank his first beer at the age of fourteen inside one of those bars. Even after the price of silver dropped, the mines stayed open. A maintenance crew, for example, continued to work. There was always money to be made, just not the amount earned in previous decades. So the mines died a slow death, and when it was happening it was described to residents as a pending Armageddon.

"It was a quiet time when the mines closed," said Mary-Lou Toly, a classmate of Gary's and a business owner since 1962 whose daughter, Roxanne, competed in the 1980 Winter Olympics in Lake Placid, New York. "I never thought Park City would get this big, that we would be from the junction into town like a big city. But we always had snow, and there were a lot of people out there who said this is what would happen one day."

In 1954, the last mining companies consolidated and became United Park City Mines, which didn't accomplish much in the mining industry. But in 1963, United Park City Mines secured a federal loan to start Treasure Mountain Resort, a ski area immediately behind the town's main street in the same aspen-choked hills where its workers used to mine. Although skiing had started in Park City in the 1920s when Scandinavian miners built a ski jump in town, it wasn't until the development of Treasure Mountain Resort that skiing officially became part of the town's future.

The $1.2 million federal loan provided a rope tow, chair lift, gondola, and several lodges. United Park City Mines urged people to hold onto their real estate because "it will be valuable one day." Not many people listened. While the resort created optimism and new jobs, the town's population hovered at eight hundred. According to current mayor Dana Williams, whose family began spending summers in Summit County in 1954, 80 percent of the businesses on Main Street were boarded up and the other 20 percent were bars. Lots with homes could be purchased for a few hundred dollars, or whatever amount was owed by the previous owners for back taxes. It became clear that the ski resort wasn't going to change things overnight.

Dana moved to Park City permanently in the 1970s. He was a twenty-year-old hippie from California who farmed alfalfa about thirty miles from town. When he came into Park City, his entertainment was sitting on Main Street, waiting for cars to drive by. Sometimes he'd sit for hours before he saw a vehicle. Most of the time, he chucked rocks into the street and then headed back to his farm out in the county. His priorities were rock 'n' roll, skiing, and partying, in no particular order. He knew plenty of kids his age cleaning toilets in lodges and sitting butts on chair lifts, jobs that ski bums had to accept. Even Gary Kimball and the former miners worked at the ski resort to make ends meet, though the miners viewed it as temporary employment because they believed the mines would eventually reopen. But they never did, and it was obvious the town's future would hinge on the success of skiing.

For the most part, skiing wasn't such a bad thing to hang your hat on in those days. Real estate was cheap and the sport showed signs of growth. Many of the ski areas in the American West had been built by 1963 when Treasure Mountain Resort opened. By 1990, all but of a few of the resorts in existence today were built. During the 1984–85 winter season, there were more than 725 ski areas in the country, but that number has dropped to less than 480 today. Small mom-and-pop ski areas have closed because they can't compete with larger ski resorts, none of which have closed since they opened for business and have only continued to expand. When it started, skiing appealed to curious athletes and was affordable to families. Heavenly Valley, for example, charged four dollars for a lift ticket when it opened in 1955. But once the creation of new resorts ceased, the sport revealed it had a ceiling, so a different set of wheels transformed these towns. In Park City, there were a series of events that turned it into an exclusive enclave, but all the events rotated around a craving for open space.

With hot-dogging popularizing skiing throughout the American West, the first major shift in Park City was the development of two other ski resorts. In 1981, Deer Valley opened, with its reputation as a skiers' only resort still intact. Deer Valley is situated at the south end of town, and when contrasted with Park City's Old Town, it is remarkably different. Instead of miner's shacks built on steep hillsides, it's a community of trophy homes and has a "members only" feel without needing a sign to deliver such a message. It's an area of 10,000-square-foot McMansions that are vacant most of the year with a second-home owner rate of more than 90 percent. These monstrosities are visible enough to appreciate their size but tucked away enough to keep gapers from getting too close. Hundreds of these homes dot the bell-shaped hill behind Park City's main street.

Later in the 1980s, Park West, now called The Canyons, opened for business between Park City and Kimball Junction. Within twenty years, the area offered three destination resorts for skiers wanting to sample the Wasatch Range's legendary light, dry powder. The claim on the state's license plate does have nuggets of truth, and ski bums in Utah certainly use quality of snow as a key debate topic when comparing their town to others.

As Salt Lake City meteorologist Jodi Saeland explains, "Most of Utah's storms come from the west and northwest. When air travels over the Pacific Ocean, it's extremely moist. Air cools as it lifts, so as the dense air passes over the West's Sierra and Cascade mountains, some of the moisture is wrung out there in precipitation. Then the storms move across the drier, colder areas like eastern Washington and Nevada, and even more moisture is essentially 'baked' out. By the time the air lifts again over the Wasatch, most of the moisture has been squeezed out of the clouds before precipitation occurs in the form of light, dry powder snow."

Another weather element that benefits Utah skiers is the "Great Salt Lake effect." The lake covers 2,000 square miles and is situated west of Salt Lake City and the Wasatch Range. It is one of the worst-smelling lakes in the country because of its high salt content. "Often the Great Salt Lake is much warmer than the bitter cold air following a cold front," says Dan Pope, another Salt Lake City meteorologist. "The lake releases water in the air that then rises into clouds of snow, producing squalls on its eastern flanks. These squalls contain some of the lightest, fluffiest, and driest snow ever produced, and it falls in feet—not inches—on our Wasatch mountains."

What the weather geeks are trying to say is that Utah has about a 6 to 7 percent moisture density compared with 10 to 12 percent in other ski regions. But it wasn't the quality of snow that attracted second-home owners and formed the resort region; it was the town's accessibility. Apart from the mines, which had workers from Kamas, Heber City, and Midway, the first modern-day example of the area's commuter culture started in 1986 when Western Airlines was purchased by Delta Airlines.

Delta created a regional hub in Salt Lake City, and almost

immediately young airline employees with three-day-on, four-day-off work schedules discovered Park City, a rather inexpensive ski town forty-five minutes from Salt Lake City International Airport. Their flexible schedules were similar to that of ski bums because it left ample time to enjoy outdoor activities such as mountain biking, hiking, and, of course, skiing. These airline workers also proved it was not only possible, but convenient, to commute from Salt Lake City to Park City. At about the same time as their revelation, Glenn Artist and Myles Rademan, who has become one of most influential civic leaders in the town's history, arrived.

Despite being in his fifties and having neatly trimmed gray hair, Glenn's boyish appearance is aided by his soft face and small, blue eyes. He was a smart ski bum who married up. He first skied in Park City in 1977 when he and a few friends traveled from California and parked their motor home in the resort's parking lot. It got so cold overnight that the water froze. Fortunately, they found the Palace Flop House, which offered showers for fifty cents and allowed the derelicts to park their motor home on the street outside its building.

While boozing along Main Street, Glenn walked into a bar bathroom and discovered lines of cocaine inside a pull-out drawer. As long as nobody was getting rowdy, cops would turn their head the other direction. Within a few years of his Park City experience, Glenn moved there for good and rented a place for $150 a month. He eventually bought a home in the Silver Summit neighborhood for $27,000. "People thought I was nuts," says Glenn. "I was the first person to buy there, and it was kind of out in the middle of nowhere. I guess I look pretty smart now."

Glenn looked really smart in 1995 when Salt Lake City was awarded the 2002 Winter Olympics, which resulted in Park City hosting the skiing and snowboarding competitions.

According to Gary Kimball, it was a good time for people watching, but it also caused a wave of trepidation. Flags from Italy and South Korea waved on the town's Main Street, and a cocktail of culture permeated the town. Park City was no longer the town of Gary's childhood. Now it catered to tourists from around the world, an interesting notion considering that just forty years earlier the town was starving to feed its own citizens.

The Olympics were the first major boom to the greater Salt Lake City area since Delta purchased Western Airlines. People who hadn't even heard of Utah learned about a once-dying mining town that had surprisingly affordable real estate for a ski town. Aspen, Vail, Telluride, and Jackson Hole were already glitter-gulch communities. Park City, though, had condos priced under $100,000 and was less than an hour from an international airport. People wanted a piece of the action, so they started buying the town's miners' shacks and then turned their attention to building homes in the Snyderville Basin.

Apart from Park West ski area, the entire eight-mile stretch from Park City's town limits to Kimball Junction was developed from 1995 to 2006, an eleven-year period that turned Park City from a ski bum haven to a mountain suburbia. Seemingly overnight, Park City became the town people couldn't get enough of. While the Olympics remain a great source of pride to Myles Rademan, who served as a torch bearer leading up to the Games, he realizes they only further disenfranchised the town's ski bums.

The Mersack Building is a cream-colored brick complex perched on a hillside overlooking Main Street and the lower reaches of Park City Mountain Resort. Myles's office is on the second floor, where many of the town's other city offices are situated.

He was doing a television interview for a Salt Lake City news channel and was late arriving to our meeting. His secretary let me into his office, where I sat waiting for him in one of the two chairs facing his desk. On the walls were pictures of Myles posing with influential people and certificates of his various civic achievements. It's not inaccurate to say that pictures covered every inch of the wall before giving way to a window that looked over Park City.

The Main Street from the old days of Gary Kimball and Dana Williams is gone. While it's still a mile-long strip that tilts downhill from the bell-shaped hill south of town—and it's still a row of two-story buildings from the early 1900s—brothels and seedy bars have been replaced by bistros, art galleries, sushi houses, and boutiques. The people strolling along Main Street are also different. Dirty miners don't hover about and ski bums aren't chucking rocks into an empty street; rather, women with fur boots stroll and families argue over what ten-dollar burger joint they want to eat at. In the summer, green tongues of grass flow down from mountaintops where there is snow in the winter, but the types of tourists don't change much from season to season.

From Swede Alley, between Main Street and the Mersack Building, the sounds of a jackhammer put the finishing touches on a parking garage. On the other side of Main Street, near where Gary Kimball lives underneath the town ski lift, a crane rises fifty feet into the sky, partially blocking a view of several ski runs. As I thought about these changes, Myles walked into his office.

He has a thick, dark mustache and a raspy, distinct voice that seems connected to a vault of experience and knowledge. We talked about the development between Kimball Junction and Heber City, how the majority of people who work in Park City don't live in Park City, and how that has stripped the town of its cultural core. He nodded and argued that I was referring to the golden age of the ski bum.

"It's a great theme for your book, and there are still places you can still go and live that lifestyle and get in on the ground floor, but you have to be willing to do that," says Myles. "We, the ski bums from the era you have been describing, were lucky because we could do both, ski and buy in at a low-enough rate. But that mentality now of 'I just finished school and I want to live in Park City,' it's like tough shit. When people say to me now, 'I want to live in Park City and I can't afford it,' I don't know what to say to them exactly. On the one hand, I want to say 'Go find some place that's not famous and make something out of it. We worked hard to make this place nice. Don't come crying to me now because you can't afford to live here.' On the other hand, if we don't have any new people coming in, we're dying. What these resort regions do is they hollow out your town. It's no longer an economic issue. It's the soul of your town you're fighting for, because nobody lives here anymore."

Ben Stevens, a ski bum in his twenties, went to culinary school in Vermont. He has lived in Park City since 2002. He's never lived outside the town limits for more than a few months at a time and now has an agreeable rental situation in town. However, his group of friends has fragmented over the years; the most recent example being a buddy who bought a home with his girlfriend in Kamas. He knows another person who bought a home in Heber City because they didn't want to get priced out of that market too. Ben, who has a simple face and cropped, dark hair, calls those towns podunk places. In Heber City, pick-up trucks towing bales of hay and tractor trailers are as common as suvs parked outside a yoga studio in Park City. Each summer in Heber, the chamber of commerce promotes the town's annual sheepdog festival, while at the same time, a symphony is being promoted in Park City.

"A lot of the workforce that is here to stay, not the people who come in for a year or two, they are buying in Heber, Kamas, or out at the junction. If they want to hold onto the lifestyle they have, they know they have to buy on the outskirts. It's kind of a zoo, really, because I have friends all over, and that takes drunk driving to a whole new level. It's safer just to stay in town."

That's exactly the situation Myles and other town leaders like Mayor Williams are trying to avoid. The city has resurrected its housing trust from the ashes and has subsidized more than four hundred units of affordable housing, which includes a mixture of rental units and home-ownership opportunities. But the rate of affordable housing units being built isn't outpacing the number of free market homes being purchased by the wealthy. Colorado's Roaring Fork Valley, where Aspen is located, has lost 60 percent of its ranchlands since the 1980s. The Snyderville Basin, where Park City rests, is on a similar path, and analysts have predicted that this current generation will be the last to witness ranching in the West. Park City's ski bums aren't really a major concern because their disappearance has, for obvious reasons, taken a backseat to other issues such as preserving open space and affordable housing for workers such as firemen, policemen, ambulance drivers, and teachers.

"These are not issues we've ducked, but I don't think you can ever solve them," says Myles. "That's like saying you're going to solve poverty or global warming. These are major issues that are beyond the capacity of any small town. As for ski bums, they are getting splintered off, but you have to look at it pretty realistically as that being part of a golden age. With everything that's happening in ski towns now, ski bums are going the way of the dinosaurs. They are becoming extinct. I can tell you why it is happening, but I can't do anything to stop it.

"The towns you are writing about are a clear reflection of what we believe in and who we are as a country. We don't follow the European model as far as development because it is un-American. They don't believe in the same things we do. They don't believe in the freedom of mobility and private property rights. In order to follow the European model, we would have to clamp down and say 'No, you can't move wherever you want. You own the property and it's going to stay a cow pasture forever.' As Americans, we don't want to tolerate that. It goes against our model of living.

"Ski bums may not like that the land around them is being bought by wealthy people and their lives are being affected because real estate values are going up, but there isn't a law in our country that says you are forced to sell your property. If someone chooses to sell because they can make a lot of money, then that's their choice. They could stay and enjoy the things they moved here for in the first place, but they haven't. The first baby boomer turned sixty on January 1, 2006, and there will be another baby boomer turning sixty every 7.8 seconds for the next sixteen years. This aging population really fueled the ski industry in the 1980s and 1990s. Now they are in their prime earning years and have inherited the greatest transfer of wealth in human history from their parents' generation. That's what fueled the real estate boom in these exceptional places. But these are mixed bags.

"Locals complain about how things don't look like they used to, but these second-home owners wouldn't have anything to buy if the original owners didn't sell their property. There is still a subculture of ski bums out there, but maybe it's getting redefined and ski bum culture has switched from Americans to South Americans and Kiwis and Aussies."

The October before my traffic jam, Myles's new breed of ski bums encountered a housing issue. It was less than a month before the ski season, and international workers from the Southern Hemisphere were wandering the streets and didn't have any clue where to live. They were told by their employers they could figure it out when they got to Park City. Lows that night dipped into the single digits. They got so desperate that these young workers from Australia, New Zealand, Argentina, and Brazil knocked on strangers' doors and asked if they could spend the night on their floor. It was a situation that troubled the mayor. Dana and I sat at a small, round table in Cow's, a coffee shop along Park City's Main Street. Ben Stevens, the young ski bum from Vermont, was working in the back. In the winters, Ben works as a chef at Deer Valley. In the summers, he works as an ice cream scooper at Cow's, which still remains Dana's favorite place to grab a cup of java.

Dana has a round face and thin, matted hair that is combed to the side. He is still a fan of rock 'n' roll and plays guitar in a local band with a strong following. He's become so popular that, in the 2002 mayoral election, nobody even bothered to run against him. Not bad for a former hippie, ski bum, and alfalfa farmer. Dana and I talked at a silver table while Ben scooped bubble gum ice cream. We agreed the American ski bum is no longer on the rise but on the decline. But, like Myles poignantly argued, Dana believes that second-home owners and resort regions aren't the only contributing factors.

"Today's ski bum is from Brazil and Argentina," says Dana. "They are doing the exact same thing we did thirty years ago, living with several people in a house and trying to make ends meet. I know resorts all over, including in Tahoe, are hiring more international employees. But these towns aren't the same as when I first moved here. They all have housing shortages."

Ski Town Invasion

The greed of gain has no time or limit to its capaciousness. Its one object is to produce and consume. It has pity neither for beautiful nature nor for living human beings. It is ruthlessly ready without a moment's hesitation to crush beauty and life.—RABINDRANATH TAGORE, winner of the 1913 Nobel Prize for Literature

I first met Keith Erickson not long after returning to Lake Tahoe from Portland, and it was impossible not to like him. Six foot five with long, blond hair that he kept wrapped in a ponytail, Keith was an all-smiles type of guy. During a break between ski towns in the 1990s, he traveled for eighteen months in Southeast Asia. He spent six of those months on a motorcycle he bought for five hundred dollars at a bazaar in Agra, India, near the Taj Mahal. After the transaction, he had a hundred dollars to his name to live off for six months.

The motorcycle Keith bought, however, didn't really fit him since it was designed for a person with a much smaller frame. His knees were positioned high above the bike's torso and they knocked his elbows whenever he encountered a bump in the road, which turned out to be quite often. Nevertheless, he steered the motorcycle through open farmland that fanned out below the foothills of the Himalaya. When the sun's rays cut through the haze, pillars of gold stretched like dominoes across a valley that was splashed emerald by the recent monsoons. As beautiful as that sight was, Keith didn't have to experience it alone. Somebody was with him.

After he bought the motorcycle, Keith felt he wasn't groomed properly for his pending journey. In India at that time, shaves with straight-edge razors cost twenty-five cents, and he decided to visit a barber. On the steps of the parlor, there was a holy man rolling joints containing tobacco and hash. Dressed in orange with dreadlocks dangling to his tailbone, the holy man asked Keith if he'd like to smoke a joint.

"Yes, I would," he said, ignoring the shave for a moment.

During the smoke session, the holy man asked Keith what he was doing in India. He told him about the motorcycle he had bought and his plans to ride into the mountains to search for a ski area near Manali.

"I'll go with you, I know the way," the holy man said.

"I bet you do because I can't read the street signs," Keith said under his breath.

In the end, they rode together for three months. They entered villages and headed straight for local markets. Keith would purchase bags of vegetables for ten cents, visit local temples, and offer the vegetables in exchange for a place to stay. Then the party really started as the holy man and temple workers rolled joints and engaged in lengthy smoke sessions. Keith, of course, participated but stopped occasionally to appreciate the interesting designs in the temple's ceilings. The Hindus felt proud when Keith took an interest in their country. He didn't speak a lick of Hindi, but his wide smiles proved to be an effective translator.

When his eyes grew heavy, Keith rested his head on the asphalt and fell into a deep sleep. He wrapped his blanket around himself in a particular way, sort of in a triangular shape that allowed mosquitoes to bite only his elbows. The holy man taught Keith such tactics, and none more useful than buying vegetables and giving them to the country's starving people. When it was time to leave for the next village, the holy man mounted the motorcycle and sat sidesaddle because of the robe tied around his waist. The position provided him relative comfort, but it resulted in him catching massive air on bumps.

After the shave, Keith returned to his hotel room to consider the holy man's offer. Several women had asked to join him on his motorcycle journey, and theirs was an appetizing proposition because vagabond traveling makes certain male body parts feel neglected. As he pondered his own desires, he recalled a recent conversation with a Canadian guy he had been hanging out with and who had visited India a decade earlier. The Canadian was reenacting a situation that made it seem like he was having his way sexually with a German girl. Keith nearly told him to stop because he didn't like how the story was developing. But just about the time he did, the Canadian explained how an Indian guy intervened and clubbed him over the head, resulting in a scar that he then flashed to Keith, who certainly enjoyed the story's ending. Their conversation then turned to the holy man Keith had just met.

The Canadian explained if he allowed the holy man to join him, he'd see the real India. But he could get into unforeseen troubles because, though widely respected, holy men are essentially glorified homeless people who wander. They do, however, know how to live off a hundred dollars for six months. Considering his financial situation, Keith was almost sold on that point alone. But before any decision was made, he wanted to bring the holy man to his room so the Canadian could meet him and give Keith his final opinion. When the holy man passed through the door the following morning, his eyes immediately connected with the Canadian's. The two men froze and the room turned awkwardly silent. The Canadian began rubbing the scar on his head, and it became clear that the holy man was the Indian guy who had clubbed the Canadian many years ago. Keith liked him already since he kept the German girl from being abused. Now it wasn't even a decision anymore; letting him come along just seemed to make sense. And off they went.

Like a rock star's girlfriend, the holy man wrapped his arms around Keith's stomach and held on tight as they ventured in tandem toward the Himalaya. Even with a 135-pound Hindu who smelled like sewage connected to him, Keith had a huge smile spread across his face. When they finally reached the ski area, Keith was approached by a man in a parking lot.

"Hey mister, mister, do you want to ski?" the man asked.

"I sure do," Keith said.

Keith, who was wearing Teva sandals, looked down at the man and noticed that he was wearing Salomon rear-entry boots and had a pair of Fischer skis that he recognized as well.

"I like those skis, and I like those boots, too."

The man jumped out of the boots and charged Keith twenty-five rupees, the equivalent of about eighty cents. If Keith had paid another ten rupees, he could get towed up the mountain behind an ox.

"No, I think I'm just going to hike," Keith said.

Attaching his boots and skis onto a makeshift backpack, he hiked for almost two hours. The ice-encrusted peaks of the Himalaya towered overhead and made him feel very small. When the altitude wore him down, he stopped on a rocky outcrop, took a deep breath, and was satisfied. The Himalaya was dramatic and larger than any mountain range he'd ever visited, basically the Sierra Nevada and Rocky Mountains stacked on top of one another. As he shook his head in disbelief, he reached into his pocket and, for a moment, his smile turned upside down.

"I brought my pot pipe, but I couldn't get my lighter to work. No expectations, no disappointments. I adopted that philosophy a long time ago. The guy who rented me the equipment was pretty mad when I got back down, thinking he was going to rent the skis for ten minutes, not two hours, but it was still a great run. I gave him back his skis, put on my Tevas, and got back on my motorcycle."

These days, Keith's smiles derive from other sources. When he lived in a different ski town each winter, it used to be that the worst part of his life was when it hadn't snowed in several weeks. But when he and his wife, Kim, and baby Zoe drove south from Mammoth Lakes on U.S. Highway 395 through the Owens Valley, skirting the immense, granite walls of the eastern Sierra Nevada, into the smog and traffic of the Los Angeles Basin, he realized that some things are more important than powder days. It was a tense drive with lots of knuckle popping and finger crossing. It started occurring about every two months during a time when Keith the ski bum was embracing his new roles as Keith the husband and Keith the father, and the drive began long before Kim's left forearm had been amputated because of cancer.

Once in Los Angeles, the Ericksons pulled their blue Subaru into a crowded parking lot, closed their eyes, and prayed their life would continue the way it had. When they opened their eyes, Keith and Kim walked side by side, with baby Zoe squeezed tight against one of their shoulders, her sparkling blue eyes the size of acorns looking out into the innocent world that remained ahead of her. Together, as a family, they entered a doctor's office to see whether test results showed that Kim's cancer had spread.

Keith grew up in Castro Valley, a suburb of Oakland in California's Bay Area. Abandoned by his dad at an early age, Keith was raised by his mother. He picked up bits and pieces of his dad's story over the years, but his mother made a point of not mentioning him often. His dad had gotten other women pregnant at an amazing clip and eventually settled in the Sacramento area. Not much else was elicited before his dad passed away, an event that caused Keith's shoulders to shrug. Though he checked in with his dad when he was alive—curiosity more than anything—as far as Keith was concerned, his dad was already dead. The funeral took place when he abandoned Keith, his mom, and five sisters, and it didn't take long for the resentment to build.

As a teenager, while his friends were riding bikes, Keith fixed lawnmowers, appliances, and leaky faucets. "This is a dad's job," Keith told himself. Paternal support would've also been useful when he was diagnosed with diabetes at sixteen. Driving to school one day, Keith passed out at the wheel. He woke up two blocks later when his friend, who was in the passenger seat, punched him in the shoulder and yelled, "Wake up, man." Keith wasn't sleeping at night and was exhausted most days. At night, he awoke every half an hour to urinate, drank a glass of water, and then needed to get up a half hour later to urinate again. When his mom heard about him falling asleep behind the wheel, she took him to a doctor's office, where he underwent blood tests. The following week, the phone rang and doctors diagnosed him with diabetes.

"That was kind of weird because I didn't know anybody with diabetes. I didn't know what it meant," says Keith, who, even in his forties, speaks in long, drawn-out syllables—a hybrid of the surfer talk Californians are known for. "The only other diabetics I knew were my friends' grandparents. That was a little depressing, like my life was ending. But in a way, it made my life more productive because I thought maybe it would be shorter than expected. I told myself 'I'm not saving for retirement. I'm going to enjoy life right now.'"

After graduating from Castro Valley High School, Keith's friends wanted to attend college and land high-paying jobs. Keith headed straight for Squaw Valley on Lake Tahoe's north shore, where he got a job at the resort and skied off every cliff imaginable. It was there, during the epic winter of 1982–83, that he experienced his first taste of the ski bum lifestyle. Snow drifts that season rose more than ten feet high and enveloped the house he and his roommates were renting. To enter the house, they had to crawl over the drifts and through the upstairs window because the front door was buried until spring. It was exciting stuff for a nineteen-year-old. He had skied growing up in Castro Valley, making the four-hour drive on Interstate 80 like the rest of Northern California does every weekend during the winter. One season at Squaw Valley, though, illuminated that driving four hours to ski is much different than waking up to it. After that, he made a goal of never driving far to ski again.

"A lot of those people I knew in high school ended up dropping out of college and, sure enough, started partying and became mechanics or whatever," says Keith. "Not that being a mechanic is a bad thing, but I was following my own dreams. They were following someone else's."

From the time the first chairlift in the United States was installed in 1936 in Sun Valley, Idaho, ski resorts have, more or less, relied on three different types of people for employment. In fact, this is true of any ski town business. The first type of employee is the retiree who's financially set and moves to a ski town, maybe has a second home there, and wants that adventurous, low-paying job they never would've taken when life was deemed more serious. These people want their youth back, so to speak.

The second type of employee is the longtime local, someone

who needs a job but who hasn't necessarily structured their life around skiing, someone like Gary Kimball in Park City. Skiing wasn't the primary industry until chairlifts were installed, and even today resorts have employees who are local residents in need of a job. When ski towns were created, these types of employees didn't migrate there because they wanted to ski. They were the children of ranchers and miners—or perhaps even the miners themselves—who came to grips with the fact that skiing was the new industry and there were mouths to feed. These first two types of employees, however, are rarely identified as ski bums.

The third type of employee is the drifter, the young and the mobile, kids who want to party and play, many of whom develop a serious obsession with skiing. Some stay for a year, others never leave. This group included Martin Hollay and the Face Rats in South Lake Tahoe, Johnny Davis in Crested Butte, and it certainly included Keith. Without a question, this third type helped plant the roots of ski bum culture.

Johnny Davis, Martin Hollay, and the Face Rats, though, moved to a ski town and stayed. Keith's settlement in Mammoth Lakes involved a more circuitous route because he adopted a system in his twenties and thirties that allowed him to sample a different ski town each winter. When the snow melted at Squaw in the spring of 1983, he returned to the Bay Area and worked a construction job that paid him twenty dollars an hour. He never officially moved back into his mom's house, opting instead to crash on friends' couches. By October, he quit the construction job with several thousand dollars in the bank, and that's when it hit him. In his mind, he had just created the ideal ski bum existence—work all summer and ski all winter. Little did he know that hundreds of ski bums around the American West already had similar revelations, but to him it was a breakthrough discovery.

The first October after Squaw, Keith drove to Jackson Hole, Wyoming, but it was too cold there for a California boy. He also found that locals were protective of the limited jobs available and weren't very welcoming. After that, he always made sure to arrive before Halloween to secure employment. He left Jackson for Aspen and skied there for the 1983–84 season. He rented a room in a three-bedroom trailer for $250 a month in Basalt, a former mining town twenty miles from Aspen, where, unlike when Johnny Davis visited his cousins in the 1970s, people were paying as much as $500 a month to live in a closet. Keith enjoyed his time in the Roaring Fork Valley, but when the snow melted it was back to the Bay Area and the same twenty-dollar-an-hour construction job. This cycle of quitting each October and returning each spring went on for five years. When it was time to leave for the mountains again, he told his boss "Good luck with the rest of the building. I'm outta here." One year, he had made so much money at the construction job that he had money left over at the end of the winter, and he decided to travel in Europe.

Europe was a much cheaper place to travel in the late 1980s, but one day Keith went to the ATM and couldn't get any money. He was broke. He had visited Turkey, Greece, and Yugoslavia but ran out of money in the Austrian Alps. His return ticket was out of London, and even though he had just landed in a ski town, he considered hitchhiking to England and returning to the United States. He decided to go for a hike to think things through, bringing his pot pipe and his lighter with him. He was on a path that was cut into the forested hills above Kitzbuehl. He came around a corner and, suddenly, something seemed vaguely familiar, like he had seen this location on television before. He looked up and saw a camera perched on a wooden platform in a tree. That's when he realized he was on the edge of the Hahnenkamm course, site of world's most famous downhill race. Keith wasn't a ski racer, but he viewed it as a sign. Just as he did in India, with the holy man who clubbed the Canadian, he followed his intuition.

"I cashed in my return ticket for three hundred dollars and next thing you know I am living in Kitzbuehl for the winter. I was pretty ignorant. I didn't care if I wasn't kosher. I'd smoke pot in the lift lines and yell at people. Europeans act a little differently at ski resorts than Americans."

He connected with the son of Toni Sailer, the Austrian ski racer who won gold medals in downhill, slalom, and giant slalom at the 1956 Winter Olympics and is an Austrian hero. Toni's son worked for the local resort and needed English-speaking ski instructors.

"Next thing you know I am a ski instructor in Kitzbuehl," says Keith, amazed at that sequence of events even though twenty years have passed.

For his living arrangements, Keith brokered a deal with two older women who were looking for someone to split wood and build them a shed. One of them had a son who was a school-teacher, a pretty boy, Keith says, who wasn't interested in manual labor. Keith built their shed and in return he learned how to speak German and got three meals a day and a bed to sleep in. Working as a carpenter in an Austrian ski town wasn't exactly what Keith had planned for when he left to travel in Europe. And unbeknownst to him at the time, foreign workers were already moving into American ski towns and shaping his future home in Mammoth Lakes. Still, he saw the merits of carpentry and started to view construction as an occupation that could keep him in an American ski town on a full-time basis. After all, Keith was almost thirty. How long can someone not have a permanent home?

He returned to the Bay Area that summer and, sure enough, got the same twenty-dollar-an-hour construction job. He skied that winter at Alta—his fifth different U.S. ski resort since graduating from high school—and returned to the Bay Area construction job for the final time the following summer. On one of his days off, he drove to Bear Valley, a small ski area in the Sierra Nevada, to participate in a mountain bike race. After the race, he went inside the lodge to watch television. Playing on the screen was a video showing people screaming down the side of a mountain with their bikes. They were riding down Mammoth Mountain.

"I was kind of hesitant to go there because, living in Tahoe, you look at Mammoth as L.A. and Southern California," says Keith. "Everyone from Tahoe kind of frowns on the place. I never even checked it out living in Squaw because we had it all in Tahoe, but Mammoth became a place where I could ski all winter and find work in the summer, a perfect combination. Alta didn't really have it, and Aspen was too expensive. I guess I could've done it in Tahoe, but I was young and wanted to see other things. I never expected to live anywhere for the rest of my life, but I think I'm going to die here."

The same could be said for Jack Copeland, who moved to Mammoth Lakes in 1973 and works as the ski resort's director of human resources. I shared several smooth ales with Jack one night on the second floor of Whiskey Creek Saloon, located at the intersection of Minaret Drive and Main Street in Mammoth Lakes. There were two pool tables behind us, occupied by men in their twenties on a quiet Friday night in December. We sat at a wooden table, Jack's stool on one side and mine on the other. A waitress with dark hair and green eyes took our orders, picked up our menus, said thanks, and returned to the bar. There was something foreign about her voice, something exotic, and later in the night I learned she was Brazilian. After seven years of living in Lake Tahoe since I graduated from college in 2000, I was accustomed to strange accents. They weren't strangers in ski towns. In fact, they had vital roles in them.

"Since I can remember being here, we've had those three groups," says Jack. "By far and away, the biggest group is the young people. We get the eighteen- and nineteen-year-olds from Southern California who are between high school and college—or high school or whatever—and we get the twenty-two- and twenty-three-year-olds that just graduated from college and are trying to figure out what they are going to do. It's just like when I came here thirty-five years ago. But when I run the numbers now, we have a different type of employee who wasn't here thirty years ago, or wasn't really here fifteen years ago. There were Hispanic workers and a few international employees, but not like we have today."

On that Friday in December of 2007, Jack said Mammoth Mountain had 261 Hispanic employees working for them, about 16 percent of the resort's 1,600 employees. Resorts today rely on two visa programs designed to attract international employees. H2-B visa workers are considered "professionals" and are typically ski and snowboard instructors from Southern Hemisphere countries such as Australia, New Zealand, and to a lesser extent Argentina and Chile. H2-B visa employees are under different requirements than those with J-1 visas, which are basically student visas for employees who are enrolled in college at home and are on summer break, which occurs during the North American winter. Jack doesn't have specific figures for the number of Mammoth's H2-B and J-1 visa employees, but there is someone who has them for all of California's resorts.

Bob Roberts is the executive director of the California Ski Industry Association, an agency that promotes and analyzes the state's ski data. He estimates about 15 percent of a ski resort's labor force is made up of either H2-B or J-1 visa workers. In the early 1990s, when Keith moved to Mammoth, Bob said they made up less than 1 percent of California's ski resort workers. Back then, resorts didn't need to use these programs because there were plenty of American employees available for hire. He also added that Hispanics weren't significant parts of the workforce, estimating they made up less than 5 percent of a resort's employee pool. During the 2007–8 season, more than 10 percent of employees at California ski resorts were Hispanic, though not every Hispanic living in a California ski town works at a ski resort.

According to a town of Mammoth Lakes housing study, 4.5 percent of the town's population in 1980 was Hispanic. By 2002, a quarter of the town's population was Hispanic, a 500 percent increase from just two decades prior.

"I would say we—the resorts in California—started in the mid-1990s bringing in these types of international employees because the great American ski bum has been disappearing off the face of the earth," says Bob. "We had a much more challenging time finding seasonal workers, so ski resorts had to start getting creative. We just weren't able to get the amount of employee support that we need to keep operations going. That was when the major resorts—Mammoth, Heavenly, and Squaw—started thinking about an international program. And it's actually worked out pretty well for us because we were able to create an interesting opportunity by packaging these H2-B and J-1 visas to get employees. As for the Hispanics, most of them are back of the house type of employees. There are lots of Hispanics working in ski towns, but they don't make up an overpowering number at resorts. In other words, resorts aren't exclusively looking to hire Hispanics. They are just part of the town now, and I think that reflects the immigration that has come into the state more than it does ski resorts targeting Hispanic employees."

Numbers suggest that the growing Hispanic population in ski towns isn't California-specific. Eagle County Health and Human Services worker Kathy Forinash told Colorado College anthropology professor Sarah Hautzinger that in Eagle County, where Vail is located, 40 percent of newborns at the turn of the twenty-first century were born to Hispanics. About three hundred miles away in southwestern Colorado, 17 percent of the Telluride R-1 School District population during the 2005–6 school year was Hispanic. The same school year in Park City, Utah, the number was closer to 20 percent, as it was for Teton County School District in Jackson Hole, Wyoming. These percentages are roughly 400 percent increases from the 1980s.

At the elementary school where my wife, Isabelle, teaches in South Lake Tahoe, about 70 percent of its population is Hispanic, with many of her kids' parents working in the casinos or other service-industry jobs. Before she was hired as a full-time teacher in Lake Tahoe Unified School District, she worked as a substitute. During one stormy week in January, my wife, who is Hispanic, asked one of her Hispanic students if they would snowboard if the district called a snow day.

"Miss, we don't snowboard," he responded.

In previous decades, Face Rats like Jerry Goodman worked as janitors cleaning toilets, as kitchen jockeys washing dishes. They were willing to take jobs below their social and skill level because they wanted to ski as much as possible. Now many of those jobs in ski towns, whether it's back of the house jobs at ski resorts or busboy jobs at restaurants, are taken by Hispanics. Some of them are here illegally, some of them are here legally, but that doesn't really matter for the purposes of this book. What matters is that Hispanics are moving to ski towns in large numbers, enrolling their kids in local schools, and taking the jobs ski bums used to take, not because they need to support a ski addiction but because they need to support their families.

In return, employers usually get much better employees than when they hired ski bums like Jerry. The most obvious reason that Hispanics are better employees is dependability. A *Los Angeles Times* article from 2004 reported that twenty-six-year-old Roberto Salazar of Kings Beach—located on Lake Tahoe's north shore—arrived every morning at a convenience store with two dozen other Hispanic men looking for work. The reporter asked Roberto if he called in sick after powder days. "No. That's for gringos. Rich gringos."

"I get calls from resorts all the time [looking for Hispanic employees]," Martha Gomez, who provides volunteer legal services for illegal immigrants in the Lake Tahoe area, was quoted as saying in the article. "Even if you have white college students coming to work, they don't stick around."

Not only are Hispanics and international employees working many of the jobs ski bums did in previous decades, they are living like them, too. Most ski bums squeeze into houses or apartments in an effort to reduce costs to minimize their time working and maximize their time skiing. Johnny Davis wrapped his house in Gunnison with plastic to survive the winter. Jerry Goodman rented a garage one season in South Lake Tahoe. Keith Erickson had six roommates in a three-bedroom apartment one winter in Mammoth. International employees are willing to put up with the inconveniences because they are usually in America for a short time. J-1 visa employees, for example, rarely stay longer than four months. Many Hispanics aren't pleased with their living arrangements in ski towns but put up with substandard conditions in order to create a life for their families.

In a 2002, the *Tahoe Daily Tribune* published an affordable housing series written by Robert Stern, whose enterprising

because they lost money doing it and started focusing on hiring international employees.

"There are some jobs where we just don't get U.S. applicants anymore," Randy Bennett, general manager of Crested Butte Mountain Resort, told the magazine. "I think American students are so in debt that they have to get into the workforce."

The article went on to state that "Foreigners appear to be the new ski bums of the global economy. This trend is attributable, in part, to the decline of the American ski bum—college kids who work in ski towns for a season or two after graduation. Also, with the cost of living in ski towns rising dramatically over the past generation, many young American workers no longer seem willing to work in low-wage positions."

Not only are second homes and resort regions affecting ski bums, but the American education system is also playing a role. In a 2006 *USA Today* article, the Project on Student Debt, a nonprofit advocacy group, said that the average student loan debt for a college graduate is $19,000—more than a 50 percent increase from the previous decade—and that many undergraduates come out of college with at least $40,000 in student loan debt. The Center for American Progress, a think-tank organization, estimates that 60 percent of college graduates have some student loan debt, and that 40 percent of those with student loan debt have what financial experts consider unmanageable debt.

In a 2007 AP article, a reporter described the situation of Kristin Cole, a thirty-year-old graduate of Michigan State University's law school, who owed $150,000 in private and government student loans. Her monthly payment for those loans was more than a quarter of her net income.

"I could never buy a house. I can't travel. I can't do anything. I feel like a prisoner," Cole told the paper.

Knowing Cole's situation—and the thousands of other college graduates just like her—there is little wonder why she wasn't at Heavenly's most recent job fair applying for a seasonal cashier job that pays nine dollars an hour. Moreover, her student loans don't reflect any credit card debt she might have. Many financial Web sites estimate that the average credit card debt for college graduates is $2,700, 25 percent of college graduates have $3,000 in credit card debt, and about 10 percent have $7,000 in credit card debt.

Myles Rademan, who lives in Park City, believes that young people in debt are contributing to the disappearing ski bum as much as a town's Hispanic population and its out of control housing situation. His son grew up skiing in Park City but was in major debt after he graduated from college. As a result, he moved to Los Angeles to start a restaurant.

"He's very serious about life suddenly, and I notice a lot of his friends are looking toward the future as well," says Myles. "That wasn't the case when I was his age. A lot of people might not want to hear this, but the young American isn't as interested in going skiing anymore. There isn't a future for young Americans in these towns anymore. My son will probably never be able to buy a house in Park City. But even if he could, the drop-out mentality isn't there anymore. It's a different world now."

In Mammoth and other ski towns, Hispanics and international employees aren't taking jobs from ski bums. They are simply filling a void left by college graduates and other young Americans who are saddled by debt and aren't willing to make the sacrifices to be a ski bum any longer. And like any smart business, ski resorts recognized this trend and adjusted their hiring practices.

"A real disillusionment has leached some of the glamour out of the ski bum lifestyle," Colorado College professor Sarah Hautzinger told the *Los Angeles Times* in 2004.

As a December sun sank behind ribbons of granite, the darkening sky mirrored a pink palette that turned into a charcoal haze. From a sagebrush field outside of Mammoth Lakes, Banner Peak, Ritter Peak, and the spires of the Minarets absorbed the day's last beams of sunlight. Mammoth Mountain, a white volcanic plug in a sea of granite, was safely tucked away for the night. The Sierra Nevada, like naturalist John Muir famously stated, is a range of light, choked with colors that have a different hue than other great mountain ranges.

Stretching four hundred miles along the eastern edge of California, the Sierra Nevada forms the state's backbone. The northern part of the range is a series of forested ridges and bucolic valleys, while the southern part has peaks rising as high as 10,000 feet above a desert valley. It's a violent piece of geology that has resulted in a spine of peaks more jagged than a shark's smile. It all adds up to some of the most spectacular mountain scenery on the continent, and it was little surprise why Dave McCoy, the son of a paving contractor from Southern California, fell in love with the place.

Dave was born in 1915 in El Segundo, a suburb of Los Angeles. As a teenager, he and his mother drove north along the eastern Sierra and visited Independence, a town near 14,495-foot Mount Whitney—the highest peak in the contiguous United States. Two years later, Dave's parents separated and he went to live with his paternal grandparents in Wilkeson, Washington, a town in the shadow of Mount Rainier. The damp charms of the Pacific Northwest didn't do much for the fifteen-year-old. In his three months there, it rained nearly every day, so he hitchhiked back to Southern California and worked in a grocery store, cut grapes, and tended pigs for room and board.

He eventually returned to Washington to finish high school and developed into a fine athlete, earning all-state honors in football and lettering in basketball and track. But it was at nearby Snoqualmie Pass, east of Seattle, where he contracted the ski bug and utilized his athletic prowess. Austrian Otto Lang had organized a ski jumping exhibition at Snoqualmie Pass, and Dave watched in amazement at the aerial display. The following winter, he made himself a pair of skis in his high school's wood shop, attached them to a pair of logging boots with pieces of an inner tube, and tried out the sport for the first time on the slopes of the Cascade Range, near where Crystal Mountain Ski Resort was built.

After finishing high school, he bolted for California, realizing that the Sierra Nevada was his calling, but he found his true calling on the trip back to Independence. He caught a ride on a delivery truck, but the driver needed to stop at Mammoth Lakes, north of Independence. The truck pulled into a bakery on the outskirts of town. While the driver completed his delivery, Dave stood outside and his eyes gravitated toward a massive volcanic plug in the western horizon, an 11,053-foot behemoth that managed to stick out among a series of much larger peaks. Even in late summer, aprons of snow continued to spill down the peak's ribs. And seventy-five years later, Dave McCoy himself became synonymous with that peak, Mammoth Mountain.

Dave eventually made it to Independence and began working as a soda jerk in a restaurant. He made himself a new pair of skis and also became friends with two men who worked for the Los Angeles Department of Water and Power, which had its regional headquarters in Independence. Among other duties, their job involved skiing in the Sierra and measuring the snowpack to predict next year's water supply for Los Angeles, which was becoming one of the country's most populated cities. Dave thought they had a dream job. In 1935, Dave and his new buddies from the water and power company built the Sierra Nevada's first rope tow out of an old truck frame and engine in Gray's Meadow. The following spring, the two men invited twenty-one-year-old Dave to join them on their next snow survey on Mammoth Mountain and, by 1937, he was hired on full-time.

"I was the one who was excited about it," Dave told Martin Forstenzer about the rope tow in the book *Mammoth: The Sierra Legend*, which provides a detailed, historical account of skiing in the eastern Sierra Nevada. "I guess I was going skiing whether anyone else went or not, and others decided to try it too."

Throughout the 1930s and 1940s, Dave built a reputation as an accomplished ski racer, winning several slalom races in California. His main training ground was at McGee Mountain, where Cortlandt Hill and Jack Northrop installed a rope tow in the 1930s. Dave made the seventy-mile drive north from Independence whenever he could. He bought a used Harley-Davidson, a purchase that continued to keep his name in the region's consciousness. With his skis attached to his motorcycle, he roared through the towns of Big Pine and Bishop, usually bare-chested and with a red bandanna tied around his head. He drove the motorcycle up and down U.S. Highway 395 to the region's ski areas. When he felt like it, he kept pulling on the throttle until he crossed the border into Canada or Mexico.

"I guess I was a character as far as other people were concerned. I was free-spirited," Dave said in Forstenzer's book.

Although there was great skiing to be had in the 1930s at McGee Mountain, locals realized that the skiing was great because they were in a cycle of consecutive big snow years. By the 1940s, the area returned to its normal precipitation and snow didn't last long at McGee. Just up the road, however, was Mammoth Mountain, which managed to remain white long after the rest of the valley had turned brown, and that's where Dave and others turned their attention. Dave had built two portable tow lifts at McGee, but when the snow grew thin, he hauled the tows over to Mammoth, where he met his competition.

Hans Georg arrived in California from St. Moritz, Switzerland, and had a modestly successful operation going on the mountain's east side. Hans's east-side location was more accessible than the north side, and he pleaded with the forest service to allow him to expand. His pleas, however, always landed on deaf ears. Dave, meanwhile, focused on the challenge of clearing roads to the north side, which received more snow and, as a result, presented more difficult access. He hired a strong, dedicated crew of young people from Southern California who loved skiing and, more important, were willing to work for pennies. Dave, it seems, had an irresistible quality about him.

"Dave was the guy who got in the ditch and dug out dirt with you," says Laurey Carlson, who moved to Mammoth in 1979 after graduating from UCLA and has worked for the resort ever since, her most current role being the resort's international recruitment coordinator. "He managed people well and was very thought provoking. He had a special quality. You learned so much about life working for him that you'd almost be willing to work for free."

While Hans put enormous amounts of effort lobbying with the forest service to expand, Dave's crew went about their business of clearing roads, building warming huts, and operating rope tows. Before long, he solved his transportation issue by purchasing vehicles that could tow people from town to the north side of the mountain. By the end of the 1940s, Dave abandoned McGee Mountain and moved his entire operation to Mammoth, enthused by a forest service agreement that allowed him to expand to the north side. He and his crew continued to clear trails and cut down trees with axes and chainsaws. By 1952, with Hans's star power fading and Dave's rising, the forest service followed through with the idea of establishing a modern ski area at Mammoth Mountain. Critics said the mountain was too remote and too snowy to attract the masses. But fifty years later, Mammoth enjoys about 1.3 million skier visits annually, making it one of the most heavily visited ski resorts in North America.

Dave held a controlling interest for all of those years, but something happened that reflected not only the changing demographic of ski towns but the entire industry: In December of 2005, Starwood Capital Group Global purchased the resort's majority interest for $365 million, just a few years after Intrawest, one of the largest publicly traded ski corporations in the country, bought part of the resort. Dave was ninety when he gave up complete control of what he built with his own two hands and decided to live out his final years near where he was born in Southern California.

"We have more people in the bathroom in a weekend than Telluride gets in an entire season," jokes Mammoth Mountain CEO Rusty Gregory. "And all of the credit goes to Dave and what he built here. He was an amazing man. Without him, there wouldn't be a Mammoth."

Without people like Keith Erickson, there also wouldn't be a Mammoth. After the December sun sank behind the Sierra Nevada for the night, I met him at his house on a narrow side street behind an A-frame liquor store. The liquor store is one of several businesses on a frontage road that parallels Main Street, which Highway 203 turns into after a five-mile drive from the junction with U.S. Highway 395. The frontage road has many of the town's businesses, a strip of development that begins at one of the town's three stoplights near The Breakfast Club restaurant. The town's second stoplight is near Whiskey Creek Saloon, where Jack Copeland and I shared beers one night. To reach the final stoplight, take a left at The Breakfast Club and you'll travel along Old Mammoth Road and through a hodgepodge of sidewalks, restaurants, and plazas.

When Rusty Gregory, Jack Copeland, and Laurey Carlson arrived in Mammoth, there weren't any stoplights. Many of the residential side streets were unpaved, and local phone numbers had only five digits. When the snow melted each spring, puddles were everywhere and the mud took months to dry. But by the time Keith moved here in the 1980s, phone numbers were seven digits and the streets were paved. The houses in Keith's neighborhood are tightly packed and protected from the sun by tall pine trees. The winter I met him, snow banks crept up the trunks of the trees, creating tunnels for driveways, which reminded Keith of his first winter as a ski bum at Squaw Valley.

As I approached town, alpenglow from the sunset had cast a creamy pink and yolk-yellow glow on Mammoth Mountain, which rises directly behind town. Despite the dwindling light, I could make out several of the thirty-four lifts that crisscross the mountain's 3,500 acres. Large custom homes have been built on the town's periphery, but the core of the town, which includes Keith Erickson and most of the working class, pretty much lives in one of several neighborhoods off Main Street and Old Mammoth Road. They are tight-knit mazes of homes and apartment complexes erected beneath stands of pine trees. Main Street connects with Minaret Road at Whiskey Creek Saloon, and a right there takes you past Mammoth's ski village, much like the Heavenly Village in South Lake Tahoe, and then to the main base lodge of the ski resort. This is where the Mammoth Mountain Inn is located and where Keith landed his first job in Mammoth as a busboy.

I arrived at Keith's two-story home after passing through one of the snow tunnels leading into his driveway. Stacks of firewood measured more than six feet high and created another tunnel-like avenue that wrapped around toward a side entrance, which I thought to be the main entrance. I walked up eight wooden steps and knocked on the door. Nobody answered. Inside the hallway were colorful Tibetan prayer flags and Indian art hanging from the wall. At the end of the hallway was a mudroom. Several pairs of skis leaned against the wall, jackets dangled from a rack that was nailed to the wall, and there was an assortment of boots on the floor. I walked back to the front of the house, where there was another door. I knocked on it. Within seconds, the thumping of footsteps got louder and louder until a tall guy with long, blond hair filled the doorway.

"Hey, Keith, I'm Rick's friend Jeremy, the guy who's writing a book about ski bums."

"Oh sure, come on in. I'm just spending some time with my daughter here."

Zoe, his eight-month-old daughter, sat on a checkered blanket on the living room floor. There were toys on one side of her but not on the other. Keith wore tan galoshes with white fur stitched above the ankle, jeans, and a faded green T-shirt with a yellow crescent moon across his left chest. When he sat down, he curled his right arm around Zoe, who proceeded to throw her toys in the air and smiled when they hit the floor.

As Keith held Zoe's back to keep her from falling, I asked him to start at the beginning, from where he was born to how he arrived in Mammoth. He gave a chronological summary of his stints in Asia and Europe, as well as his system of working all summer and skiing each winter. There was, however, a part of his story I didn't hear until his wife, Kim, walked through the door. When Zoe saw her mom, she crashed onto the floor.

"Wipeout," Keith responded.

"Hi, pumpkin," Kim said to Zoe, picking her up with her right arm.

Kim was diagnosed with fibric sarcoma soon after she and Keith were married, and doctors had to amputate the lower part of her left arm to keep the cancer from spreading. The family's monthly drives to Los Angeles to see if the cancer has spread are no longer necessary, and they go only occasionally as a precaution. If that's an example of beating the odds, it must be a personality trait because Kim and Keith ending up together was a long shot.

They met at Idyllwild, a rock climbing spot in Southern California, and Keith convinced her that day to move to Mammoth, where they began dating. Everything was fine until he told her he was leaving to travel in Southeast Asia.

"Then I went on a dating spree. I would just date so many guys," Kim said as she turned her head toward Keith.

"I knew I always loved her," Keith replied a bit sheepishly. "When I got back, we kind of picked up right where we left off. I definitely thought about Kim a lot, saying to myself 'She is a pretty cool girl, really. I never felt like that toward any girl before.'"

Despite her dating spree and Keith's vagabond traveling stint, Kim still fell for him, though she didn't know exactly what she was getting into. Like most other single guys in Mammoth Lakes, Keith was a ski bum, and marrying a ski bum is different than dating one. It requires an ability to overlook the fact that your husband might not be a pillar of stability. For example, when he was hired as a busboy at the restaurant inside the Mammoth Mountain Inn, Keith worked swing shift, cleaning tables at night and skiing during the day. After just a few weeks on the job, his boss was so impressed with Keith's work ethic that he offered him a promotion.

"Keith, you're good. We want you to be a waiter. You can make more money," his boss said.

"Okay, what's the schedule?" Keith asked, probing to make sure nothing interfered with his skiing.

"Well, you'll be working the mornings and afternoons," the boss replied.

"That doesn't sound like a promotion, dude, I'll just stay as a busser."

So imagine the dilemma Kim faced when the prospect of marrying Keith presented itself, but there was something about Keith that she was attracted to, notably his zest for life and his good heart. She took the plunge and couldn't have known at the time what a great father he would become. As Zoe was pressed against her mother's chest, Keith grew excited when she said something to the effect of "doggy." It wouldn't have been confirmed by a linguist expert, but, to Keith, when she said doggy, it was a beautiful thing. He dreams about getting invited to Zoe's house for Thanksgiving one year or Max's, the couple's second child. Keith also can't wait for family ski days on the mountain.

"When I was traveling in Europe and Asia and moving around each winter, I never thought I'd be where I am today, the family man, but I've done the ski bum thing," says Keith. "You have to embrace change, and you have to plan for the future a little. I work more now, and Kim works a little less to watch Zoe. But she works just enough as an aide at the hospital to keep health benefits so that our family is covered. And having a dad with diabetes, a mom with cancer, and two kids, we can't be without health insurance. That is something you don't think about when you are twenty. We were fearing life a couple of years, and now we're a happy family. It's just another step in life, but it was like I was saying before. I've done the ski bum thing. I've slept on couches, slept in my car, lived with eight people in a two-bedroom apartment. At some point, if you want to ski the rest of your life, you can't be a ski bum anymore. You have to be a serious skier. That's what I tell people now. I'm not a ski bum. I'm a serious skier."

Kim, still standing near the front door with Zoe held tight against one shoulder, rolls her eyes, looks over at me, and says, "He's a ski bum. Don't let him tell you any different."

My next visit to Keith's house was the final one. We sat at his kitchen table and drank a few beers. The living room was still filled with Zoe's toys, though some of them had successfully made their way onto the kitchen floor. Keith stepped around them with little difficulty, pulled open the fridge, picked up two beers, and handed me one of them. He explained to me that he and Kim bought their house for a sum of money he still shakes his head at in disbelief. The second floor of the home has two units that they rent out to offset costs.

"It's a big mortgage, but it's kind of like the whole roommate thing as a ski bum. The lower your overhead, the more you can ski. If you get enough people in here, it becomes affordable for all of us. That's what international kids are doing now. That's what a lot of people have to do now to live here."

Like he did in Austria and the Bay Area, Keith works construction. He's honed his skills enough to where he is responsible for many of the custom homes built on the periphery of Mammoth Lakes, the McMansions that brush up against the granite wall of the Sierra Nevada. Being in the construction industry, he comes across more Hispanics than he did when he first moved to Mammoth. And being that he skis a hundred days a year—even as a family man—he's noticed that, more and more, the people who scan his season pass at the resort are foreigners with accents and wear name tags with home countries of Chile, Australia, or New Zealand etched into them. When he first moved to Mammoth, the places etched into those name tags were Escondido, Huntington Beach, and Fresno.

"Jeremy, do you want another beer?" Keith asked.

"I'd love one," I responded.

Keith reached for a small first-aid kit and placed it on the table. He opened a latch, pulled out a needle, and inserted it into his bicep. "I have to take a couple of units of insulin if I want another beer," says Keith. "Anyway, about what you were talking about before. Yeah, the town has changed and our individual lives have changed. But, again, you have to embrace change. I think it's great that there is a chance Zoe might learn Spanish while going to school here, and I'm jealous that she'll be able to go skiing after school. Those aren't things I could do growing up. I was too busy fixing leaky faucets and lawnmowers. The other day I was up on the mountain and everybody was excited about being out there, and that's when it hit me. There might be different people in this town now, but it's still about being around people that are so passionate about something. You know, most people aren't passionate about anything. They work their nine-to-five and drink their beer when they come home or whatever. Living in a ski town, you're surrounded by people who are passionate about something, whether it's skiing or snowboarding or climbing. All the towns I've lived in have changed, but while it lasts it's cool to be around people that are so stoked about life, and you kind of feed off that energy.

"You're not thinking about skiing when you're up there . . . you're kind of in your own little daydream. Sometimes I imagine I'm in an Indy 500 car and I'm hanging onto turns and going as fast as I can. Life can be screwed up. Sometimes you can't help what hand you are dealt, but you can still make whatever you want to out of it. A lot people think 'Oh, you're

not going to ski as much when you're married and have kids.'
Well, yeah, I don't ski as much as I did when I was nineteen,
but I'm still skiing and will ski for a long time. At the same
time, Kim knows what puts a smile on my face, and skiing
is one of those things. And she knows that if I'm happy then
our whole household is happy. In my opinion, if people are
doing what makes them happy, then they are living life right
and they got their priorities straight."

Before I walked through Keith's front door and drove back
to Lake Tahoe, I looked back at his living room. Zoe was rolling
around on the floor, and Keith was leaning down to join her.
Over his shoulder were his jacket and skis in the mudroom,
still dripping with melted snow from his day skiing on Mammoth Mountain. Keith, like many ski bums, has his priorities
straight, but skiing is not the priority of everyone involved
in the industry.

Resorting to Madness

If Telluride ain't heaven, then heaven can wait.

—DIZZY GILLESPIE, Jazz artist

Ping, ping, ping.

Jack Carey, resting on a bed of leaves with his girlfriend's naked body on top of his, will never forget that sound. Of all the noises that day—the moans of his girlfriend as she rocked back and forth, the slapping of her flesh against his, the hiss of wind passing through the aspens—he still remembers that sound. On an afternoon stroll, Jack and his girlfriend stopped on the side of a hill to make love in the sunshine. They were kissing, satiating their desires.

Ping, ping, ping.

Below them, the San Miguel River meandered through a valley filled with aspens and conifers. Telluride, which had less than a thousand residents at the time, was as tranquil as it was secluded, situated at the end of a box canyon. When Jack first visited, he turned off a highway and was told to drive three miles on a spur road and that he'd run into a town that might interest him. The year was 1975, three years after Chicago native and Beverly Hills entrepreneur Joe Zoline opened Telluride Ski Resort with financial backing from Switzerland firm Simonius-Vischer. Joe and his wife, Jebby, descended upon Telluride in 1968 and agreed it had seen better days. The Zolines had owned a ranch in Aspen since 1955—nine years after Chicago businessman Walter Paepcke founded Aspen Ski Company following World War II—but the two towns were nothing alike. Aspen had a prestigious think tank called The Aspen Institute, art and music festivals, and an established ski area that hosted an International Ski Federation (FIS) race in 1950, an event that gave it a world-class reputation within the global mountain community.

When the Zolines arrived in Telluride, the town's population was five hundred. The Ghost Town Club of Colorado made frequent expeditions to the San Juan Mountains and considered including Telluride on its list. Most residents were miners down on their luck or hippies who had found somewhere to squat. After the town was founded in 1878, mining was the primary industry until a labor dispute in the early 1950s resulted in the loss of several hundred jobs overnight and nearly gutted the last of the town's mining population. Telluride was originally named Columbia, but with so many other towns named Columbia, residents wanted to avoid confusion and changed it. The minerals extracted from the area consisted of gold, silver, lead, and zinc. Ironically, the metal tellurium, which is where most believe the town's name was derived from, isn't on the list. Others, however, believe its name came from the phrase "To hell you ride" alluding to the town's remoteness, which can't be debated.

About 350 miles from Denver and 500 miles from Phoenix, Telluride has never been easily accessible by car. Regardless of the origination point, it's only reachable by driving over several mountain passes and on state highways that rank far down the priority list when it comes to the state's budget. Despite its remoteness, the town saw its population swell to five thousand during the mining era, more than twice its current population of twenty-four hundred. But when the Zolines got there, most of the buildings along Colorado Avenue had been boarded up. Abandoned miners' shacks and rusted tailings littered dirt streets and the surrounding hills, which suited hippies just fine but nobody else. In the 1990s, the forest service conducted a sweep of these decrepit shacks and discovered people were still living in them. Other creative folk made their homes in ice caves during the winter and teepees or tree houses during the summer. Nevertheless, it was a dying community when Joe and Jebby arrived and a risky place to start a business, especially one as audacious as a ski resort. Joe, though, looked past the challenges and saw one of the greatest mountain amphitheaters on Earth, one that held great potential for development, tourism, and commerce, and he was right in one respect. Telluride has the number one rule in real estate on its side—location, location, location.

On his drive in that day back in 1975, Jack Carey wanted to believe there was a town, he really did, but it seemed as if the road would end where the valley met a cathedral of cliffs and tumbling waterfalls. Oh well, he figured, he'd reach the dead end, turn around, and drive back to the highway, continuing on with his life as a victim of a nasty prank. No way was there a town back here, he kept telling himself. Then he crested a small rise and, sure enough, a meadow gave way to rows of shimmering, pitched rooftops, a grid of dirt roads, and a main street lined with Victorian homes. Jack saw the same boarded-up buildings and dilapidated mining shacks that the Zolines did, but he too saw potential. Jack tilted his head toward the sky and noticed a ring of 13,000-foot peaks, the same peaks he saw driving into the valley. Looking at them now, however, caused a slight pain in his craned neck. The mountains were imposing and had an addictive, magnetic quality.

"When I saw this valley and these mountains, I wasn't leaving," says Jack.

Not long after his revelation, Jack was on a hillside making love to his girlfriend. Birds chirped from tree branches. Rapids curled over boulders in the San Miguel River as it flowed toward the Colorado River. The tedium of his teaching career and hurried pace of mainstream American life, he had decided, were worth sacrificing to be part of this mountain symphony. But on that day, when his girlfriend was riding him underneath a brilliant sun, the mountains were so quiet that, almost four decades later, he yearns for the chance to hear that sound again.

Ping, ping, ping.

"To be in this valley, and be out hiking and doing your girlfriend in the hills, and hearing that hammer from a guy working on his barn, it was a beautiful thing. It was magic," says Jack. "Now all you hear is the hum of everything: the traffic, the people, the machinery. We just build and develop, build and develop. If there was an off button, I'd press it."

There isn't an off button in ski towns, Jack has learned, only on buttons.

On the Vail Resorts, Inc., home page, there are images of what I'd expect from one of the world's largest ski corporations—mountains, skiers, and snowboarders, a stand of aspen trees. Then there are images of golf courses in the Colorado Rockies and of beaches in the Bahamas. As the pictures change, the message stays the same: "Extraordinary Resorts, Exceptional Experiences." I am confused as to why a ski company would promote exceptional experiences at golf courses and beaches. To help resolve my confusion, I watched the 2006 documentary, *Resorting to Madness: Taking Back Our Mountain Communities*, a film produced by skiers Hunter Sykes and Darren Campbell.

The film starts out predictably enough. There's a clip of a

skier carving a powder line down a mountain and then pictures of scenic mountain locations. After that, Hunter and Darren get down to business. No longer are there pictures of fresh snow, lakes, and sunsets, but of bulldozers, cranes, multi-storied commercial buildings, and an interstate twisting through the Colorado Rockies. A former ski and mountain bike instructor for Vail Resorts at its flagship Vail Mountain, Hunter is the narrator and takes viewers around the nation. Supported by footage of rampant development and interviews with industry advocates, the film's premise is this: The current generation of ski resort owners—in particular Vail Resorts, which owns Heavenly in Lake Tahoe, and Intrawest, the majority owner of Mammoth—aren't solely involved in ski towns because they care about skiing, snowboarding, or the communities they do business in. Above all else, Hunter argues, they care about one color, and it's not white.

"You have to keep in mind that most of these corporations are owned by Wall Street," Hunter tells me in the Lake Tahoe home he rents. "Vail Resorts, for example, 95 percent of its stock is owned by a dozen huge fund groups such as Morgan Stanley. They are simply looking for a return, and they don't give a damn about what happens to these towns. If you look at the executive level in Vail Resorts, the overarching umbrella is that all the executives are in the hotel industry, the cruise industry, the resort industry, the rental car industry, the insurance industry. None of them are skiers. We didn't intend to make Vail look bad in the film, and the reality is we could've covered most every major ski resort owner in the country and came to the same conclusion. It's what people are calling the 'Ski Areas Arms Race.' Even the small ski areas are doing it because they know if they don't keep up with the big guys—Vail, Sun Valley, Deer Valley—they will go under. This arms race is everywhere, and it's insidious."

I conducted a routine Internet search that revealed the backgrounds of Vail's board of directors, which makes the important financial decisions for the company's shareholders, and Hunter is right. They all held prominent roles for our country's biggest corporate players before joining Vail Resorts. Prior to being named Vail's chief executive officer in 2006, Rob Katz worked for Apollo Management, a private equity firm with offices in New York, London, and Los Angeles that had roughly $16 billion invested in companies around the world in 2008. Shortly after his hire, Rob, who made $3.53 million in 2007, was profiled in newspaper articles that were accompanied by pictures of him skiing. On his first day with Vail, he announced that the company's corporate offices were moving from Avon, a mountain community ten miles from its flagship resort, Vail Mountain, to a 56,000-square-foot building in the Denver suburb of Broomfield. It made perfect sense to Rob, who was living a few minutes away from Broomfield in Boulder.

Journalist Lynn Bronikowski wrote in *ColoradoBiz* in 2006 that Rob "did it without hesitation, knowing from a business standpoint it was better for the company to operate out of a metropolitan area near business and transportation resources than tucked away in Avon, outside Vail."

"Change is tough, especially when there's a perception that it's made for you," Katz says in Lynn's article. "People were taken aback because where you live is important in people's lives. You can have all the business rationales in the world, but we didn't try to tell people they are going to like this news. The first day was the worst, but within a month or two, the move had receded as an issue and I've witnessed a reinvigorating of excitement of people's careers."

That's an interesting summation to Hunter because, while many people moved to keep their jobs, he estimated that the office lost 25 percent of its workforce since several long-time employees refused to leave the mountains. After all, the resort's business offices had been in Eagle County since 1962, when Vail Associates was formed by Pete Siebert. Pete was a former member of the Tenth Mountain Division who returned to the United States after World War II and worked as a ski patroller in Aspen. In 1996, the company was renamed Vail Resorts, Inc., and a year later, with the help of Apollo Management, it was publicly traded on the New York Stock Exchange. Not long after, Vail, Intrawest Corporation, and American Skiing Company were all publicly traded companies, a trio of conglomerates that author Hal Clifford called "The Big Three" in his book *Downhill Slide*.

"None of Vail's executive-level employees have ever lived in a ski town, other than when they were forced to live in Avon for a year, which they hated," says Hunter. "They lost long-time employees who moved to Vail and loved it there. But they didn't want to move to Broomfield, and they didn't. Vail Resorts didn't care. They went anyway and lost some really good people. That shows you their attitude."

Judging by the resumes of Vail's board of directors, it's clear why Rob Katz wouldn't let a few disgruntled mountain folk dictate company policy. While it's hard to imagine Dave McCoy, who was an avid skier, moving Mammoth's business offices to Los Angeles because his investors didn't want to live in—or commute to—Mammoth Lakes, Rob's decision to move the corporate offices should have been interpreted in this way: *It's not 1962 anymore, and I won't act like it is. Our company is not going to grow by selling five-dollar lift tickets and two-dollar hamburgers.* If Rob's decision wasn't interpreted that way, then the lineup of associates he surrounded himself with certainly should have been an indicator that Vail was no longer treating skiing as a cottage industry.

Before being appointed to the Vail Resorts board of directors in 2008, John T. Redmond was affiliated with MGM Grand Resorts in Las Vegas from 2001 to 2007 and before that Caesars Entertainment. Keith Fernandez, president of Vail Resorts development since 2006 was formerly president of a privately held real estate firm in San Diego and Hawaii, where he was a landowner and developer. Stanley D. Brown, executive vice president and chief operating officer, joined Vail in 2007 after working for Marriott in various capacities since 1989. Thomas D. Hyde was appointed director in 2006; he previously held executive roles with Walmart Stores, Inc. Joe R. Micheletto, chairman of the board, joined Vail in 1997 and held executive roles with Ralcorp Holdings, Inc., one of the world's largest producers of cereal and other food products, and before that was vice president and controller of pet food company Ralston Purina. Board director John F. Sorte's experience before joining the Vail Resorts board was in investment banking. William P. Stiritz has been a private equity investor since 2001 and before that worked for Agribands International, the overarching umbrella for Ralston Purina and Ralcorp Holdings, two companies where he also served as chairman. Roland Hernandez has a background in the MGM Grand entertainment company, the Ryland Group home manufacturing company, Walmart, and Lehman Brothers Holdings, one of the world's original and most successful investment banking firms before it filed for bankruptcy in 2008, an announcement that sent shock waves throughout the world and severely dented the U.S. economy.

The trend continues at Booth Creek Holdings, Inc., the nation's fourth largest ski company. More than half of its executives previously worked for Vail and have either investment banking or real estate development backgrounds. Before being acquired in 2006 by privately held Fortress Investment

Group, LLC, and taken off the New York Stock Exchange, Intrawest had a board of directors with similar resumes. When companies are run by these types of people, skiing obviously isn't solely about recreation.

Vail Resorts, Intrawest, Booth Creek, Inc., and POWDR—the four largest ski corporations in North America (American Ski Company dissolved in 2008)—are money-making machines engineered by a who's who of corporate America, because skiing is big business. And like other small businesses that attracted deep-pocketed investors to take the company to another level, the ski industry is learning that corporate America keeps score by dollars, not powder days. Families such as the Muellers (Crested Butte) and the Kemmerers (Jackson Hole) might not mesh with the corporate suits in the board rooms at Vail or Intrawest, but they are competing in the Ski Area Arms Race. Vail, Intrawest, Booth Creek, and POWDR might be more visible players, but every ski resort is being forced to make decisions in light of this reality: skier numbers are stagnant.

Skiing's popularity in the United States peaked in the 1980s when there were an average of 50 to 52 million annual skier visits. In *Downhill Slide*, Clifford wrote that two key factors responsible for skiing's growth are now contributing to its stagnation, the more influential of the two being the baby boomers. They are the generation of 78 million Americans born between 1945 and 1964 that inherited the greatest transfer of wealth in our nation's history. And it was in the 1980s and 1990s when baby boomers were the beneficiaries of a unique way of life, and skiing was part of it. Not only were baby boomers at their peak physical condition in the 1980s, they possessed a rare blend of financial and physical prowess that made ski vacations a reality. It was practically their birthright as Americans.

Baby boomers are the result of the end of World War II when there was a noticeable spike in the birthrate in English-speaking countries such as the United States, Australia, England, and Canada. When men and women in these countries reunited after a long war, it didn't take long for seeds to be planted. This postwar sex-capade created a much different society than was in place before the war. As toddlers, they were the first generation to grow up with televisions. As teenagers, they were the first generation to view rock 'n' roll as religion. Many of their parents lived through the Great Depression, but baby boomers became disciples of the country's first widespread consumer culture. With the expansion of television and radio, businesses had more effective ways to promote their products. As a result, baby boomers became targets of mass marketing—both in products and lifestyle. Both *Time* and *Newsweek* published articles about how corporations viewed baby boomers as the engines of a growing economic vehicle.

During the 1950s, baby boomers witnessed the Ford Thunderbird introduced as our country's first luxury vehicle, Elvis become the world's first rock star, and the formation of Motown. In the early 1960s, a million baby boomers went off to college. Freshmen were tossed into cramped dorm rooms and lounges, creating a crush for student housing on campuses that continued every fall for the next two decades. By the mid-1960s, universities started graduating the largest senior classes in history. After receiving their diplomas, college-educated baby boomers entered the workforce, and they purchased more cars, clothes, real estate, and vacations than any other generation before them. They also valued time off. People living in areas with ties to recreation industries believed this new breed of Americans created an opportunity, and it's no surprise that every major ski resort in the country either formed or expanded after World War II. The building of new ski resorts continued unabated until the 1980s, when something happened.

Hal Clifford wrote that in 2001 40 percent of people who consider themselves skiers in the United States earn more than $75,000 annually, and that the household median income of skiers was $91,400. These figures fall within the nation's middle- to upper-class income bracket, and his reasoning for such high salaries is strictly because of baby boomers—not Face Rat Jerry Goodman making eight dollars an hour working ski patrol. He theorized it wasn't an accident that the last two major ski resorts built—Beaver Creek, Colorado, and Deer Valley, Utah, which happen to be two of the more exclusive ski resorts—both opened in 1980, when the oldest baby boomers were thirty-five. Clifford also provides statistical evidence that people who consider themselves skiers participate less and less in the sport by the age of forty-four. And, on average, 10,600 baby boomers have been celebrating their forty-fourth birthdays every day since 1989, meaning ski resorts are losing their most reliable customers year after year.

Resorts hoped that snowboarding, which became a mainstream winter sport by the late 1980s and was a hipper alternative for the 46 million Generation Xers born between 1966 and 1979, would fill the void left by aging baby boomers. Snowboarders provided an initial surge, but they only replaced a small percentage of those skiers who were responsible for the sport's decade of peak popularity in the 1980s, and they never had the wealth their parents did. The end result is that the average number of skier and snowboarder visits nationwide between 1997 and 2008 was 55 million, essentially the same amount as the 1980s when only skiers were at ski resorts. That doesn't even take into account population growth as there were 238 million people living in the United States in 1985, compared to 305 million in 2008.

"People in the ski business are trying to figure how out to make money," Clifford told Hunter and Darren for *Resorting to Madness*. "There is less and less opportunity to make money selling lift tickets. What I saw when I was researching *Downhill Slide* was the evolution of a new business model. In the '80s, you started to see a flattening out in the number of skier days. When you get an industry like that, whether it's sales or automobiles or skiing, you start to see consolidation, and I think this is the critical twist. They aren't trying to make money in a meaningful way on lift tickets. They are trying to make money on all the stuff that surrounds the ski area, in particular real estate."

According to the National Ski Areas Association, in the United States there were 481 resorts operating during the 2007–8 season, down 35 percent from a record high of 727 in the 1980s, and the closing of more resorts seems inevitable. The four largest ski corporations in North America own or have business interests in 27 ski resorts, roughly 4 percent of North America's 770 resorts that operated during the 2007–8 season. Yet they account for nearly 35 percent of the 73 million skier and snowboarder visits in North America. So not only is the ski industry experiencing a closing of resorts, it is watching four corporations monopolize the mountains. And although there are an increasing number of small investment groups that have purchased ski areas in the twenty-first century, their behavior isn't any different. When there is a stagnant customer base, businesses act like piranhas. They don't eat each other. Instead, they fight over a finite amount of food left in the river, effectively starving a segment of their species. The less aggressive piranhas, which usually mean family-owned ski resorts, don't stand a chance because they have neither the power nor the capital to compete. Eventually, history has proven, they get swallowed up or disappear.

"We're competing against work, we're competing against the local athletic club, we're competing against the Internet," Andy Daly, former president of Vail Resorts, told Clifford in *Downhill Slide*. "We compete against the other ski resorts, but we really also compete with Las Vegas, against the warm-weather resorts, the cruise lines. We're competing for people's leisure time, and people are working more instead of less."

Vail Resorts, in particular, will go to great lengths to compete for people's leisure time, and it doesn't always play nice with those who tarnish its image. When Hunter approached Vail Resorts for *Resorting to Madness*, it declined multiple interview requests because it felt there wasn't an upside in participating. Vail stated that because of the documentary's premise, it would be in a defensive posture and would be forced to defend itself from environmentalists and others who have been critical of the company's pro-expansion business model. Nevertheless, Hunter pleaded with Kelly Ladyga, the company's director of corporate communications, to arrange an interview. Vail didn't budge, and e-mails between the two parties turned nasty. Unable to crack the layers of Vail's corporate structure, Hunter went with what he had, and the end result was a one-sided depiction of Vail Resorts, as Hunter had feared. But Vail's combativeness with the media isn't anything new.

In 1996, Bob Berwyn began working as a reporter for the *Summit Daily News*, based in Frisco, Colorado. The paper's coverage area includes Vail-owned resorts Keystone and Breckenridge. Bob's reporting beat was the ski industry. Before diving into the beat, he was told by an editor that high-ranking employees of Vail Resorts frequently called to complain about stories that were perceived by Vail as being anti–ski industry. In Vail's eyes, Bob was told, anti–ski industry articles could range from opponents of resort expansion to environmental impacts in the national forests where Vail's ski resorts are located. During his first three years with the paper, Bob would wake up at night and wonder if stories he had written would result in him getting a call the next day from Vail Resorts.

"It got to the point where it became a real stressful situation for me, personally," Bob told Hunter while being interviewed for *Resorting to Madness*. (The part of the interview about being pressured by Vail Resorts never made it into the film, but Hunter provided me video footage of the entire interview.) "In the end, in 1999, I was told by my editor that I would be taken off the ski area, ski industry beat, and they offered me another one that they said was equivalent, to cover business and some other stuff. I feel that was a direct result from pressure from the ski industry. I feel like, as a journalist, that you got to be very careful. I think you should be objective, but the pressure is definitely there. I feel that if I write a story about a ski industry proposal or a proposed expansion, just by bringing up subjects like water quality or lynx or so forth, it's perceived as being a negative to the ski industry, by the ski industry. I feel like they really want glowing stories. I don't feel like they want an open discussion of these issues. And it's not just the press. I've heard of cases where forest service personnel have been pressured by ski industry lobbyists and attorneys."

Bob switched to business, but he eventually returned to the ski industry beat. When he did, the pressure resumed. On November 19, 2009, Bob wrote a column for the *Summit Daily News* about how the industry exaggerates snowfall totals and purposely misleads people in the hopes that it attracts more customers. In the column, he wrote, "Take, for example, the October storm on the Front Range when Vail Resorts eagerly announced that it shut down its headquarters because the heavy snow was so terrific. What the company didn't mention is that its offices are in low country in Broomfield, 75 miles from its closest slopes, where it was warm and sunny that day. I sometimes wonder whether the ski industry wouldn't benefit more from being completely transparent about weather and snowfall with its customers. But when snow = money, perhaps that's expecting too much."

Bob's editor, Alex Miller, read the column and approved it for publication. Within two weeks, Bob was fired. It was reported in the *Denver Post* on December 10 that Vail Resorts CEO Rob Katz had called *Summit Daily News* publisher Jim Morgan after the column was published and voiced his displeasure with Bob's remarks, but things quickly escalated. According to the *Denver Post*, Vail Resorts temporarily canceled its ads with the paper, a severe financial blow to a small-town newspaper during a time when Reno, Nevada–based Swift Communications, Inc., the parent company of the *Summit Daily News*, was hemorrhaging employees because of declining ad revenue. Bob had survived the massive layoffs, but the *Summit Daily News* was operating with a skeleton staff, so it seems unlikely that it fired him for something other than what happened after his column was published.

It was obvious to Bob that he wasn't another layoff victim, partly because Swift had previously laid off people in simultaneous waves but mostly because the stench was different. He felt there were other factors at play, specifically money and power. Vail Resorts is Summit County's largest employer, with nearby Keystone and Breckenridge providing thousands of jobs. With the threat of losing advertising dollars from its most important client, which could paralyze a paper that was already crippled, publisher Jim Morgan called a meeting with Alex and Bob to discuss the matter further. At the meeting, according to Bob, Alex and Jim asked him to "grovel" with Vail Resorts.

"I told them I don't grovel and left the meeting," says Bob. "Later I found out that I had been fired. I don't have a problem with Rob calling me and complaining, or calling the publisher and complaining. In fact, I expect Rob Katz to call and complain. He's been doing that for years. He's trying to protect and stick up for his company. What I didn't expect was what my employer did. I expected them to back me up, which is what they had done in the past."

When I talked to Bob the week after the *Denver Post* article was published, he was being inundated with interview requests from state, regional, and national media. A *New York Times* reporter interviewed him and asked whether he wondered if Vail did this because it was aware newspapers were suffering and that it would force his publisher to make a critical business decision, not a journalistic one.

"I had to tell the reporter that I couldn't comment on that part of it because I don't know much about the financial part of newspapers or how any of that works. I am just a reporter, but now that I think about it, yeah, it wouldn't surprise me if some of that is true."

"It's unfortunate but, especially in this economy, some advertisers feel like they can flex their muscles when there's commentary that they don't like," Ed Otte of the Colorado Press Association told Susan Greene of the *Denver Post*, the reporter who broke the story about Bob being fired.

When Greene's column was published, damage control was already underway at both the *Summit Daily News* and Vail Resorts. *Summit Daily News* publisher Jim Morgan published an exclamation for Bob's termination:

The reason Berwyn was terminated—and I have to be careful here because it is a personnel issue involving an individual—was not because of the column or because of the resulting fallout from it. In the great scheme of things, the column in question (about weather) was actually somewhat benign. Threatening to cancel ads is often the way advertisers flex some muscle and make a point. That sort of thing happens with big advertisers and small advertisers, frankly, all the time. It's part of the business we're in. Interestingly, we've had advertisers now threaten to cancel ads because of Greene's column. As would be the case with any employee, if there are circumstances symptomatic of a pattern of behavior documented in reviews over the course of time, then changes result.

What was interesting about Jim's explanation is that he alluded to newspapers having to routinely deal with advertisers threatening to cancel ads. But when I approached Vail Resorts for comment, communications director Kelly Ladyga rejected that claim. I also asked if Vail Resorts calls and complains to media outlets when they report unfavorably about her company. She sent me this e-mail response within an hour of my request:

As you know, there are literally hundreds of stories each year in each of the *Vail Daily*, *Summit Daily*, and *Tahoe Daily*, and other media outlets that are critical of our Company. Every now and then, our Company may call the media outlet to express concerns about unfair treatment, or lack of balance or inaccuracies in reporting. . . . Our Company has never threatened anyone's job because of a story we don't like and this incident was no different than any other. Rob did not threaten anyone and certainly did not intend for Bob to be fired. If he had, he certainly would not have called Bob to discuss the issue. He called because he has worked with Bob in the past and was under the assumption that he had a good enough working relationship with

Bob to have a frank discussion—and because the Company would need to continue to work with Bob going forward. However, this is where things went awry.

Vail Resorts, though, became concerned with the growing story when Dave Rossi, a Breckenridge town council member, posted on Twitter sensitive information that it felt only Rob Katz, Bob Berwyn, and Jim Morgan should have known about. Vail was under the assumption that the private conversations between Rob and Jim—and Rob and Bob—were confidential, but somehow Dave got wind of the banter and commented on Twitter. It was apparent once Rossi tweeted that Rob's assumption of confidentiality was incorrect. Rob then felt it was necessary to defend Vail Resorts on his personal blog, which stated:

> A few days later, Dave Rossi tweeted about my call to Bob Berwyn and Jim Morgan and the substance of the calls. This was very distressing to me as I felt like either Bob or Jim or both had broken a confidence and were now re-broadcasting our private conversation before we had even had a chance to talk further about the issue. It was at that point that we decided to put a temporary hold on our advertising, until we could get a better understanding of what was happening. We did not discuss this decision or the reasons behind it with the *Summit Daily*. Our company advertises in numerous publications locally and around the world, many of whom publish articles we don't like. However, we expect the media companies we work with to have an appropriate channel to discuss the issues we might have with any part of the publication. In this case, we didn't have the opportunity to do this. I cannot stress enough that our Company never threatened the *Summit Daily* in any way either about Bob Berwyn or about our advertising. We

made a business decision due to significant concerns with our business relationship. Our company highly values our relationships with the media and fully respects the need for reporters to maintain objectivity and independence in their stories. However, like anyone, we expect that we will be provided an opportunity to express our concerns and that they will be received with the utmost professionalism. We understand that the media has the right and obligation to hold us accountable, but we also believe the media needs to be held accountable as well in how they treat the subjects of their stories.

This same language was woven into a press release that Kelly continued to refer to when I pressed for specifics of the situation. What was odd to me, however, was all of this transpired because Bob implied that Vail Resorts wanted to make people think that it was snowing at its ski resorts and didn't clarify that it was actually snowing in suburban Denver—not in the Rocky Mountains. Such deception would only result in increased lift ticket sales and other on-mountain sales such as food and beverage.

But in an industry with a stagnant customer base, resorts aren't even surviving—let alone growing, a staple of capitalism—by selling lift tickets. In 2007, for example, Vail Resorts revealed in its annual report that lift ticket sales accounted for only 30 percent of its total revenue, a figure that includes season pass sales and daily lift tickets purchased. The rest came from real estate, lodging, and other on-mountain services. Even that percentage seems to be on the high side because in 2008 the company reported total revenue earnings of $1.15 billion. For the 2008–9 season, Vail Resorts generated $91 million by selling 204,000 season passes, which equated to roughly 8 percent of its total revenue earnings from 2007. By comparison, Vail Mountain Club at the base of the company's Vista Bahn lift generated $70.1 million—or 6 percent—in private membership fees alone.

Tracking the behavior pattern of baby boomers, Vail Resorts needed to offer more than skiing. It needed to be an option when an Arkansas couple made its vacation plans. Sitting on a chairlift when the temperature is five degrees, however, isn't everybody's idea of a vacation. To become an option, Vail had to get creative. It had to diversify. Vail and other major ski corporations are using a business model that Joe Zoline envisioned and that Ron Allred and Jim Wells—Telluride's next owners—perfected. It's a model that a remote town such as Telluride needed to remain competitive with more accessible resorts, but now it's a model most ski resorts are using to stay in business. Basically, Vail, Intrawest, Booth Creek, and POWDR had to start offering "Extraordinary Resorts, Exceptional Experiences."

"The mom-and-pop places that opened, they just wanted to provide a service," Lisa Schmidt, executive director of Save Our Canyons, a Salt Lake City–based environmental group, said in *Resorting to Madness*. "They wanted to make a decent living. It was for their community . . . they had a couple chairlifts. Now look what you have. You have resorts that are completely catering to people that are not living in this area. You're looking at a winter industry and now you're seeing what can we do in the summer? How can we bring more people in for conferences? How can we build a golf course? It makes no sense to build a golf course in an area like this."

In 1969, the U.S. Forest Service notified Joe Zoline that his permit application to build a ski resort in Telluride had been approved. In February of 1972, forest service representatives walked into a crammed Nugget Theater and announced that the resort would start by building five ski lifts. Joe employed a local miner and local skiers Emile Allais and Billy Mahoney Sr. to help assess terrain and cut runs. The resort didn't open until December of 1972, but real estate values jumped 150 percent in a month. The spike in home prices didn't really equate to much money since Victorian homes that sold for $3 million in 2008 could be purchased for a few thousand dollars in unpaid property taxes in 1972. The properties' previous owners had abandoned their homes and left town. Still, local residents rejoiced in the first positive economic news in decades. Within a six-month span, the town's population nearly doubled as people flocked to the rugged San Juan Mountains for newfound employment opportunities.

Of course, it didn't take long for miners and skiers to clash. Newmont Mining, an international gold mining company that owned numerous tracts of land in the area, understood that mining wasn't part of the town's future. But with the opening of the ski resort, it had an opportunity to use its property holdings to develop and ride the wave of the future. Newmont, though, needed someone to facilitate its real estate transactions, and that person was Tom Watkinson Sr. The Watkinson family moved from New York to Telluride in January of 1974, when son Tommy was three and the ski resort was in its second winter of operation.

Tommy remembers mining trucks rumbling through the streets and creating plumes of dirt. Although mining had been scaled back, the mines were still operating when the ski resort opened, and housing was tight. Miners usually were brought in by the busload from surrounding towns. In grade school, Tommy thought it was entertaining when ski bums with skis slung over their shoulders passed groups of grubby miners at the end of each day. Neither of his parents were skiers, and their family was one of the few that had a father who worked and a mother who stayed at home. They owned a house on the corner of Spruce and Columbia, a Victorian built in the late 1800s. Most families needed both parents working to get by, which meant the Watkinson house became the town's unofficial day care in summer.

Tommy's mother would make dozens of sandwiches and send the kids into the streets with full bellies. His parents often got calls from the drugstore because their son had ordered so many ice creams that his debt needed to be resolved. When the family dog, Sundance, jumped over the fence in the front yard, Tommy whistled to bring him back. The town was so quiet that Tommy could whistle from anywhere in town, and Sundance would find him within minutes. Across the street from the Watkinson house was a field where children played kickball, baseball, and rode BMX bikes, the usual stuff kids do growing up. But it was when the Watkinsons visited other parts of the state that they realized how off the grid they were.

In Denver, they'd write checks at stores and cashiers would get puzzled looks on their faces and ask, "Where is Telluride?" By the time he was in high school, his parents felt their kids had experienced enough. The enrollment at Tommy's high school in Grand Junction was greater than the population of Telluride. The decision to move had a lot to do with Tom Watkinson Sr. being outspoken and involved with local politics. He was on the school board, and being a lawyer for one of the town's largest mining companies spurred consistent reaction from dissenters. They were in a no-man's land, but not just geographically; they weren't part of the mining community or the skiing community. And with ski bums and hippies—or "flower children" as Tom Watkinson Sr. referred to them—becoming more of a presence, they realized that they were city folks living in a small town and that it was time to leave. Tommy's parents didn't approve of their impressionable children being surrounded by the characters who were gravitating to Telluride. Their disapproval, though, didn't erase their son's memory because Tommy certainly remembers "Wacky" Jack Carey.

"There is a difference from the skiers then and now," says Tommy, who lives in Ridgeway with his family and works in the ski resort's marketing department. "Wacky Jack Carey is an obvious example. He was part of those young people who were happy to be out of college and then go right back to dormitory life. Not many people are willing to do that anymore, creating bedrooms out of closets. I think it's a different type of ski bum now. They are still there, but how they are pulling it off is not the same as how they used to pull it off. You got to be a little more serious to be a ski bum now. It's a different animal now. Society has changed so much in the last twenty or thirty years, and it's a different world and the ski bum is different. The word *bum* is not the right word anymore. You can't really be a bum and live in Telluride—or any of the great ski towns—anymore. Now you have to work two or three jobs and ski a few days a week instead of every day. Maybe you have to be a telecommuter and just be happy about getting on the hill as much as possible. Or maybe you have to be the guy who takes a week off to go heli-skiing in Canada. Maybe that's a ski bum. Whatever it is, there aren't too many Wacky Jack Careys anymore."

One afternoon in March of 2006, I met Jack at Chair 8, a bar at the base of Telluride Ski Resort. It was warm for that time of year, with hints of spring emerging from winter's grasp. The San Miguel River flowed around snow-covered boulders; melting snow created coffee-colored streams in the streets, and the valley floor revealed patches of dead grass. I was working for a ski town newspaper at the time and convinced my employer to send me around the American West to write a series of stories. With my reporting complete for the Telluride part of the series, I was late for a meeting with Jack. If I didn't get to Chair 8 by 4:00 p.m., it might be tough to find him in the throng of people enjoying après-ski beers.

"Don't worry, you can't miss him," a female employee at the San Miguel Housing Authority assured me after my final work-related interview. She was right.

Jack was waiting for me at a black table on the patio outside Chair 8. The sun was setting over the peaks above us, but the temperature was tolerable. He wore black ski bibs, with suspenders and a gray undershirt, and had a long beard. No, he had a beard not many men will ever have, the type you grow in prison just to see if you can. It was grayish with brown streaks, and it nearly reached his belly button. He was balding but had hair flowing down the sides of his head. On his weathered hands, he wore a ring with a silver eagle. He had blue eyes and a set of raw teeth, with gold caps on several of them. It was like he had never given up Halloween candy and chewed tin foil for breakfast. He was perhaps the most interesting-looking man I have ever seen, and he likely would've been any town's most famous resident.

Growing up in New Hampshire, Jack skied but focused on basketball once he entered fifth grade. At six foot four, I had no reason to question him. He attended Keene State College and began teaching there after graduation. Living on the Atlantic Coast, he drove every winter weekend to ski. He often visited North Conway in New Hampshire's White Mountains, but he mostly skied at Maine's Sugarloaf, where his brother worked and where he had a friend who was an accomplished mogul skier. Part of his brother's job was to film the resort's top mogul skiers, and watching such high-level athletes stoked a desire in Jack. He didn't start out as a great skier, but once he skied moguls with his buddy, he proved to be quick learner.

"I learned enough to know that I didn't want to ski in the East," says Jack.

During his summer break from teaching in 1972, he drove west. When he reached Snowbird, Utah, and saw the steep walls of the Wasatch Range and Little Cottonwood Canyon, it was game over.

"I sent in my teaching resignation right then."

He made his way to Steamboat Springs, a remote town in north-central Colorado, and skied there for two winters. It was in Steamboat where he also developed a passion for hang gliding. But when a hang glider was killed one day, the sport was outlawed in that part of the state. It didn't take long for Jack to hear about Telluride, where it seemed nothing was illegal. He arrived in 1975, the third year the ski resort was in operation, and he, too, noticed a rift between the skiers and miners.

"The natives were pretty straightforward and hard-working miners who didn't understand the hedonism of the ski lifestyle," says Jack. "Just like people in ski towns now, they didn't like that their town was changing. In that respect, the ski bums had more in common with the hippies. The miners were chasing the drugs to confiscate them. We were chasing them as well, but not to confiscate them."

The 1998 movie *Scrapple* is, in my opinion, the most accurate depiction of Jack's existence in Telluride during the 1970s and early 1980s. Interestingly enough, the fictional town of Ajax is the movie's setting, but anybody who's been to Telluride knows it was filmed there. Mountains are like fingerprints, no two are the same, and Telluride's are as distinct as any found in the world. Ajax is also the nickname for Aspen Mountain.

The plot revolves around a pig named Scrapple that a group of stoners captured in the spring. Their plan for Scrapple is to care for him throughout the summer, then sacrifice him during an autumn roast in honor of the snow god Ullr. I won't ruin the ending for you, but the main character is some pinhead named Al Dean, who wears tight, colorful sweaters and has a serious afro for a white man. He's a small-time drug dealer who picks up his shipments at the post office and tries to avoid the one sheriff in town, who is as incompetent as Al. Plus there's an unscrupulous real estate broker who wants a piece of Al's drug business. The real estate broker entices Al by assuring him a great price on a house located on Spruce Avenue. Al's prize shipment is a bunch of Nepalese Temple Balls, and their reputation has the town's recreational drug users, who happen to be all of his friends who also wear hideous sweaters and polyester sport coats, bursting with excitement.

While anxiously waiting for the delivery of the Nepalese Temple Balls—and Scrapple's sacrifice in the fall—Al and his friends play baseball in meadows and drink cheap beer on lawn chairs. They ride beach-cruiser bikes around town, play pool in saloons, have parties on decks of cabins, and generally do, well, nothing. It's a fairly accurate and fascinating portrayal of Telluride's . . . err, Ajax's, kicked-back lifestyle, and I have been told it's more entertaining under the influence of marijuana. Ajax's understaffed law enforcement agency is also comparable to Telluride's in the 1970s, and Jack and his friends liked it that way. What they didn't like was Glenn Frey's 1984 hit single "Smuggler's Blues" about the growing drug trade in the United States, and in particular Telluride's role. The song describes drug smuggling in the 1980s, and how drugs such as hash and cocaine were stashed in Telluride after moving through Miami and Los Angeles.

"That really pissed us off," says Jack. "We didn't need that. Yeah, it was happening, and it was fantastic. The redneck cop, when we all came in, was trying to catch us. What eventually happened was that all the ski bums got together. We actually got candidates on the town council, and they got elected because they outnumbered the old miners. There were still cops. You couldn't light up in front of them, you had to show some respect, but you could walk down an alley or stand in front of a bar at closing time and smoke a joint. Nobody was going to mess with you. Coke was a different story. It was a little harsher, but it was just as prevalent. You could leave a tip for a waiter and leave a big, fat line in a cup."

I don't know why ski towns developed a reputation for strong drug cultures, though it's likely a perfect storm of factors—remote locations, limited law enforcement, residents and visitors who like to recreate, visitors who have money to spend, and residents who need to make money. But no matter how laissez-faire drug use might have been in the eyes of law enforcement early on, that's changed as much as ski bums and ski towns.

In 1989, South Lake Tahoe mayor Terry Trupp was arrested in Operation Deep Snow on charges of conspiracy and money laundering in connection with cocaine sales and a smuggling operation. Nineteen Lake Tahoe residents, including several doctors and real-estate brokers, were also arrested in the sting. Although the sheriff in *Scrapple* is an idiot, that isn't the case with San Miguel County sheriff Bill Masters, who moved to Telluride in 1974 and got a job working as a lift operator and trail builder for the ski resort. In 1975, he was hired as deputy marshal for the town. A year later, he was appointed chief marshal at the age of twenty-four. In 1980, he served his first term as county sheriff. Seven terms later, he's still the county sheriff. He's the editor of *The New Prohibition: Voices of Dissent Challenge the Drug War* and the author of *Drug War Addiction: Notes from the Front Lines of America's #1 Policy Disaster.*

Bill became a leading expert on drugs by developing his chops in drug-infested Telluride in the late 1970s and 1980s.

Drugs are still available there, but it tends to be on the lighter side like marijuana and magic mushrooms. Cocaine? You'd be hard-pressed to find a ski town without it. I have a friend who ski bummed in Aspen in the 1990s and oftentimes was exhausted working his night job as a waiter at an Italian restaurant. When his boss noticed a lack of energy among his employees, they were encouraged to walk into the bathroom where several lines of cocaine would be waiting for them. Reputations, though, don't disappear overnight. In 2005, Telluride nearly voted to pass a proposal that would've made possession of an ounce or less of marijuana the town's lowest law enforcement priority. The final tally was 308 for the proposal and 332 against it. A libertarian, Sheriff Bill Masters told the *Telluride Daily Planet* newspaper that marijuana prohibition should end statewide and nationwide, but he didn't want San Miguel County as the place to start that change.

"If you want to change the law, don't do this stuff per community, go and change the law on the state level," he told the paper. "It's a mistake to have our community be singled out as the one that allows that. We don't want people coming here because they can smoke marijuana."

While the hippies, ski bums, and miners did their thing, Telluride was also doing its thing, which is to say it was greasing the wheels of change. The ski resort might have been the town's first economic vehicle in decades, but it only drove the local economy for part of the year. From April to November, a lot people went elsewhere for work. To stabilize its economy, Telluride began organizing music, film, and arts festivals and is now the state's unofficial summer festival capital. There's even a No Festival Weekend in September when local residents celebrate the fact that, for the first time in months, there isn't a festival. The ski resort, though, was the only thing going in the early 1970s. The first three years the ski resort was in operation, it didn't connect to town. Skiers had to drive seven miles through Adams Ranch and then take several lifts to reach the resort's summit. Most locals, though, took a public bus in the morning and skied outside the boundary lines back into town at the end of each day. By 1975, Joe Zoline had built the Coonskin lift that linked the town with the main part of the ski resort, which until then was hidden several thousand feet above the Victorians along Colorado Avenue.

In 1978, Joe sold Telluride Ski Resort to Colorado natives Ron Allred and Jim Wells. Childhood friends who had gone their separate ways—Ron was working as a dentist in Colorado Springs and Jim as a certified public accountant in California—they were considering new career paths when they reunited in 1973. Jim was nearly finished overseeing the merger between Getty Oil Company and Tidewater Oil Company when Ron wooed him into commercial real estate development. The timing of Ron's proposal couldn't have been better. Jim had grown tired of working seven days a week, and this merger would be his last. Before venturing into ski town real estate, they developed six professional office buildings, two apartment complexes, and a shopping center in Colorado Springs.

Within a year, Ron was out of dentistry and turning his attention to the Interstate 70 corridor. Jim and Ron bought some land in Avon, west of Vail, and conceptualized a master-planned community with amenities that would be the first of its kind in the Rockies. Their vision paid off as they leveraged that property at the base of what would become Beaver Creek Ski Resort in 1980 and had enough capital to create the top resort in North America in Telluride. Ron and Jim recruited Dave Flatt, another longtime friend who had extensive experience in development and finance. All three played in Telluride prior to becoming owners of the ski resort, but none of them were serious skiers. They were, however, pro-expansion businessmen. Damn good ones, too.

Incorporated in 1995, Mountain Village spreads across 3.3 square miles on the relatively flat western shoulder of Telluride Ski Resort at an elevation of 9,600 feet, nearly a thousand feet above the town of Telluride. If the views from town blow you away, try to absorb them from Mountain Village. To the west, 14,017-foot Wilson Peak anchors the Wilson Massif in the Lizard Head Wilderness. When viewed from the east or north, Wilson Peak's pyramidal shape has become the iconic symbol for the Coors Brewing Company's advertisements. In every other direction, jagged peaks rise above mountain valleys, making it the ideal location for Ron and Jim to develop Mountain Village.

"Looking at it now, it seems like things happened overnight, but they didn't," says Jack Carey. "It was slow, gradual growth. The mountain was being developed, but it never got overcrowded and the runs stayed in good shape. More people were finding ways to make a living here, and that's when this community of climbers, skiers, or whatever was really created. We just figured this was the maturation of it all. Nobody could've known what it would eventually become."

Immediately after acquiring the resort from Joe Zoline, who retained a minority interest, Ron and Jim devised ways to build the area's bed base. Telluride didn't have many lodging options for tourists—at least not on the scale Ron and Jim were interested in creating—so they developed Bachman Village, a group of condos that provided as many "pillows" as already existed in town. Then they invested nearly $4 million into Telluride Regional Airport, which opened in 1985 on a nearby mesa, land that Allred had leased from sheep rancher Albert Aldasoro. On November 6, 1984, Telluride voters overwhelmingly passed (379 to 134) a $1 million bond to help build the airport. Allred had convinced the town's residents that having commercial airline service would make Telluride—and what would become Mountain Village—more accessible and allow it to compete with Vail and Aspen. It wasn't really a tough sell since locals were aware that day-trippers would never expand the ski resort since, well, Telluride will never have that many day-trippers.

In 1984, the closest towns of any size—and by size let's say 8,000 people—were Grand Junction (128 miles) and Durango (118 miles). Instead of making the two- to three-hour drive to Telluride, Grand Junction residents could drive one hour to Powderhorn if they wanted to ski, while Durango residents could drive forty-five minutes to Purgatory (now Durango Mountain Resort). Montrose, which was best known for having the closest stop light to Telluride at sixty-six miles away, only passed the 10,000 population barrier in the late 1990s. Montrose is where Telluride residents shop because it has national chain stores such as Wal-Mart. And unless they want to spend four dollars for a can of tomato soup, it's also where they grocery shop. Now the nearest stop light is thirty-eight miles away in Ridgway, population nine hundred, where Tommy Watkinson and his family live.

"The people who come here now, they want things we never dreamed about," longtime resident Linda Miller told the *Telluride Watch* newspaper. "For instance, it's really a treat to go down to Montrose to grocery shop. But now people are talking about 'Oh, we need a big grocery store here, and we need this here.' Not the innovative things, they want the mainstream things."

Ron encountered minimal public outcry with the airport

and his other development plans. The airport, though, was a pivotal point in Telluride's timeline, not only because it's the highest commercial airport in North America at an elevation of 9,078 feet, but because it was a means to an end. Ron gladly accepted the public's vote to pass the airport bond but he was building one regardless. He already had landing strips in mind for a private airport when he agreed to partner with the local government and promoted it as a win-win for everyone. Ultimately, the airport acted as the middleman linking Ron and Jim's baby—Mountain Village—with the outside world, specifically those who could afford to buy what would be offered there. Jack Carey certainly wasn't who Mountain Village was intended for, and it was built with that kind of mentality.

Designed to accommodate 7,000 high-end residents and vacationers—triple the amount of the number of residents and pillows in Telluride—Mountain Village was born in the early 1980s, and Ron, Jim, and Dave decided that $12 million was needed to get started. The trio began acquiring tracts of land in the Adams Ranch area, and they each assumed specific duties. Jim attracted an investment group and bankers. Ron dreamed up the amenities and conveniences that the village's residents and guests would expect for the prices they would be paying. Dave, meanwhile, completed the village's first residential project. Mountain Village was established in 1987, two years after the airport opened, but the action that immediately followed its official introduction to the world was the selling of subdivided residential lots. A major turning point came May of 1992, when the first hotel opened for business.

The Doral Resort and Spa, now named The Peaks Resort and Golden Door Spa, is a 177-room hotel carved into a stand of conifers on the hulking western shoulder of the ski resort.

At a cost of $100 million, it was so grand that nobody noticed until it was too late that its height of 130 feet surpassed the county's height limit by 40 feet. It didn't matter. It was perfect, the most extravagant ski resort luxury property in our nation's history. The *Telluride Daily Planet* estimates that the hotel's winter guests pump $4 million into the ski resort and even more into the area's airlines, shops, and restaurants. That summer, Telluride Golf Course opened and Telluride Ski Resort was renamed Telluride Ski and Golf. Now the area could offer golf in addition to summer festivals during the offseason.

"I have no idea how skiing got connected to golf," says Glen Plake, a South Lake Tahoe resident and one of the world's best-known skiers. "Skiing is a hick sport where you drive to the end of a road, go to the top of a mountain, deal with cold weather, and work hard to get back down. Golf is a sport where you wear short sleeves and drive around in a cart when it's warm outside. Those are about as extreme opposites as you can get, but somehow it's happened."

In 1994, Telski established its corporate offices in Mountain Village. And in 1996, Telski opened its $19 million gondola that transports visitors and residents between Telluride and Mountain Village in twelve minutes, the first free transportation system of its kind in North America. Since the Doral, other large hotels have been built in the village, most notably the marble-floored Fairmont Heritage Place, Franz Klammer Lodge. There are condos splintering in every direction from a chaotic blend of cobblestone and shop-lined alleyways in the heart of the village. But most of Mountain Village's 3.3 square miles consists of single-family homes, and just not any type of single-family homes. Linked to the resort by strategically placed lifts, they are the kind of homes part-time residents Tom Cruise and Oprah Winfrey consider suitable "vacation" properties. Oftentimes when driving Mountain Village's streets, it can be difficult to decipher what's a hotel and what's a residence.

"The people that drive all of these places are baby boomers buying the real estate," says Hunter Sykes. "I think the interesting point will be when the baby boomers are done buying all this shit and they can't buy anymore because they are dead. That's going to be a huge issue because, I think, you're going to have towns that literally collapse. You'll end up having the ghost town cycle all over again like how these towns collapsed after the mining bust. But what's worrisome to me is that the infrastructure in these towns is much more permanent than anything built in the mining days. The fallout of this could echo for hundreds of years down the line. It will have that kind of impact because all of these towns are located in sensitive environments. And as these towns get developed, there are all sorts of conflicts of interest going on. One of the biggest problems with municipalities is that elected officials all have that one thing that sways them. It might be free golf or a helicopter skiing trip. But for the most part, it's tax money, tax revenue. They sell it to residents by saying it's going to be great for your economy, but we all know what it really does. It drives up the value of real estate and brings in more tourist dollars and creates more tax dollars. There is still mining being done in mountain towns. It's just the mining of the tourists' money."

Mountain Village may have earned the distinction as Colorado's newest municipality in 1995, complete with a pharmacy and post office—and even fire and police departments—but don't be fooled. Mountain Village, which has a second-home ownership rate of 80 percent, was the first master-planned ski village in the United States; it is one every other major ski resort developer on the continent has emulated in one form or another, not necessarily in terms of design, but in functionality. It also achieved another first in state history by becoming the first municipality to pass a law through the state legislature allowing non-permanent residents to vote in local elections. That ensured that the full-time population, which is dominated by low-wage earners living in employee housing, doesn't shoot down ballot items that might thwart the village's pro-development mindset.

It doesn't matter where you visit—Squaw Valley, Vail, Mammoth, South Lake Tahoe, Jackson Hole—the foundation of American ski villages is that they are trumpeted as European-style. I've been to Switzerland, and none of our villages are like Zermatt, Gstaad, or Engelberg. When I visited Les Diablerets, children pelted one other with snowballs after school. A couple divvied up the errands at the end of the day, with the man going to the bank and the woman going to the market. There were families dining in second-floor restaurants and laughing under candlelight. When they finished, a man draped his wife's coat over her shoulders as they walked through narrow streets back to their house. This wasn't some vacation purchased on the Internet and packaged with a bow; it was their life. In Mountain Village one winter, I remember a kid yelling "I want to go home" to his dad who was fumbling the family's assortment of ski equipment as they walked toward their condo. When he looked over at his wife, who wasn't carrying any equipment and was staring at necklaces through a jewelry shop window, he heard "Honey, we should have just taken him to DisneyWorld."

The cobblestone pathways, tight streets, no vehicle traffic allowed signs, chocolate shops, South Americans on student visas working in cafés, none of it had anything on Mickey Mouse. Ski villages in America are like boat docks for cruise ships. Tourists arrive one weekend, spend a bunch of money over the next seven days, and then leave the next weekend when a new batch of tourists takes their place. Our ski villages are successful from a developer's point of view, but think of them as gardens with constantly blooming flowers and without any gardeners, soil, or roots. What makes a great garden is the person who takes the time to properly mix the soil and care for it with regular watering. The end result is a beautiful flower with colorful petals that should be enjoyed, but the process that produced the flower is what's truly admired by others. Americans are willing victims of instant gratification. Want to lose weight? No problem. Forget exercise and dieting, take a pill. Want to see the Eiffel Tower? Don't go to Paris, go to the Paris Hotel and Casino in Las Vegas. We even build stuff we already have. Want to see the Old Faithful Geyser erupt? Don't go to Yellowstone, go to the Wilderness Lodge at DisneyWorld in Orlando.

Yet, tourists come in droves. Blame Ron and Jim for that. They were ahead of the curve. They knew people wouldn't come to Telluride just to ski, and that was when skiing was at its peak popularity. Now other ski resort owners are creating their own extraordinary resorts, exceptional experiences because baby boomers aren't interested in skiing any longer, but ski resorts still need their money.

When skiing was at its peak in popularity, the image of colorful characters living a simpler life was hijacked by marketing gurus and prostituted to sell the mountain lifestyle. That's why ski resorts in the 1980s and 1990s primarily focused on advertising their expert terrain. They had commercials showing well-tanned men with pretty women behind them skiing moguls on thirty-five-degree slopes. They had middle-aged adults in ski bibs and turtleneck sweaters enjoying cocktails in lodges by a fireplace, snow melting off their ski boots from the fire's radiant heat. As baby boomers have aged, ski resorts have changed their tactics. Now they advertise more comforting aspects such as intermediate terrain, high-speed chair lifts, and grooming machines. When they promote off-mountain amenities, it's often with images of women receiving massages with rocks placed on their backs. I must hand it to them. Ski resorts and real estate developers have taken one of the most frustrating vacation experiences and made them desirable. They don't advertise whiny kids in the back seat of the SUV as daddy drives them over a mountain pass in a snowstorm. Or the long lines at the check-in counter at the airport. Or the long lines at the rental shop. Or the long lines at the lift ticket window. Or the long lift lines at the resort. Or menu prices for a bread bowl or a hamburger. It's all about "Extraordinary Resorts, Exceptional Experiences."

In the 1970s, Adams Ranch was pristine wilderness where Rocky Mountain elk roamed. Now it's a village at the base of one of the continent's top ski areas—with terrain that can rival any resort's. But it's still 350 miles from Denver and 500 miles from Phoenix, and somehow it competes with DisneyWorld, Hawaii, and the Grand Canyon. Two words sum it up for resort owners and developers such as Jim and Ron: mission accomplished. They sold a majority interest of Telski in 2001 to Hideo Morita, a Japanese businessmen and son of Sony founder Akio Morita. Not unlike what Hunter and Darren predict in *Resorting to Madness*, which argues that major ski corporations simply mine ski regions for money and move on when profit margins disappear, Jim and Ron cashed out and moved on.

"Hey, we needed growth to sustain the town and keep the lifts moving," says Hugh Sawyer, who moved to Telluride in 1980. "When rich people go on vacation, they need people to help them out, and that's where we come in. A lot of local skiers and ski bums, they couldn't adjust fast enough and we lost them . . . we lost some of our town's soul. We didn't know all this would happen. We're now a resort town, not a ski town. Resort towns are no longer about skiing. That's because skiing is hard. It takes muscles. Telluride's an advanced mountain. It's a hard place to get to, and it's a hard place to ski. You don't have a golf cart that takes you down the hill. A lot of families don't like it, but they like the other stuff, and that's what keeps us a resort town and keeps me able to live here. I just got here early enough where all of the stuff that happened here didn't drive me out. Others weren't so lucky."

Jack Carey wasn't driven out for the reasons Hugh mentioned, but he disappeared nonetheless. In July of 2009, Jack was cycling near Lizard Head Pass, where he collided with a truck and was killed instantly. He was sixty-four. According to *Powder* magazine, the ski resort will name a tree run in his honor.

"Losing Jack was like a building in town being torn down—something that was there forever and is now gone," Tommy Watkinson told *Powder*.

Here's the thing. Ski bums are indeed disappearing because of the reasons that I've mentioned: An increasing immigrant population, second-home owners, ski towns becoming resort towns and resort regions, and ski resort owners focusing on amenities other than the sport itself. All of these trends drive up real estate values and cause ski bums to reevaluate their situations. These reasons, however, are just symptoms of capitalism that are affecting every corner of the country. If it seems like ski towns are evil places, I apologize. They aren't. Like anywhere else, they are full of business people making business decisions. And in a capitalistic society, if a business isn't growing, it's dying. Until now, my intention was to provide a background on the evolution of mountain communities whose local economies were stagnant and rejuvenated by skiing, the interesting characters who helped turn them into ski towns, why ski towns morphed into resort towns designed for tourists, and the people left behind in their wake. That much is clear, but what might not be clear is this—skiers and snowboarders are better than ever.

Swift, Silent, Deep

The tradition of respect, even admiration for individualism, is still very much alive in Jackson Hole. Unlike many other communities, large and small, where the pressures to conform are intense, here to be a maverick is not be a pariah.

—ROBERT E. BETTS, *Along the Ramparts of the Teton*

Wyoming's Teton Range peels back from Jackson Hole with unmatched bravado. America's other great mountain chains have allowed room for dense forests and foothills to be part of their landscape. Not the Tetons. As one of the youngest ranges in North America, they had neither the time nor the desire to wait for others to catch up, employing a topographical survival of the fittest. In an aggressive race to the heavens, they rise an uninterrupted 7,000 feet above a valley inhabited by elk, moose, and bears, but ultimately it was Grand Teton that stood tallest. At 13,770 feet, it's the centerpiece of the forty-mile-long range and one of the highest points in the Rocky Mountains outside of Colorado. Like an Olympic podium, the others flank the Grand in descending order of height. The French, though, didn't bother ranking the Tetons. They simply described them and did so with little tact.

Eighteenth-century French trappers were the first white men to see the peaks, viewing them from the west. They called the South, Middle, and Grand Tetons *les trois tetons* which, in English, means "the three breasts." Hopefully they hadn't seen women for a long time and their imaginations were running wild because, if women's breasts in Paris look like the Tetons, then the French really are assholes. Big breasts, however, have always been admired by men, so perhaps it wasn't a shock when President Teddy Roosevelt saw the Tetons and announced, "This is how mountains are supposed to look." More than one hundred years later, he's still right, and there's no amount of silicone that can make the Ozarks look like the Tetons' Cathedral Group.

The Cathedral Group is technically Grand Teton, Mount Owen, and Teewinot, spires exploding from the same granite chunk, but the group is generally considered the high points between Cascade and Death canyons and comprises eight of the tallest peaks in the range. When seen from the northern reaches of Jackson Hole valley, the Cathedral Group looks like a set of ruffled, granite curtains hanging from an invisible rod, placed there by mountain deities who discovered after centuries of trial and error that perfect mountains would be part of what would become northwest Wyoming. Glacier-carved canyons bisect the north-south range, a horizontal succession of incisions that left behind natural scars in the form of rock buttresses and complex cliff patterns within each deep cleft. But it's a mountain south of the Cathedral Group, one that hasn't appeared in an Ansel Adams landscape portrait, that matters most to ski bums. More than anywhere else, Rendezvous Mountain, the home to Jackson Hole Mountain Resort and the continent's most notorious ski fraternity, is a proving ground. In the real world, they say if you can make it in New York City, you can make it anywhere. In the ski town world, that place is Jackson. Not coincidentally, at the bottom of Rendezvous Mountain is the office for Teton Gravity Research, a film company started in 1996 by four Jackson ski bums who parlayed a $15,000 investment into a million-dollar enterprise.

"TGR is responsible for an entire movement," says Howie "Hollywood" Henderson. "The type of skiing you see today, the types of things you see in ski films today, the money you see people making in skiing today, TGR is responsible for that. TGR—and the skiers they started filming—had the balls to start promoting themselves. There were others, of course, but the boys from TGR were the first skiers—not someone who owns a ski resort or a hotel at a ski resort—but the first really great skiers to show up here in Jackson and say 'You know what? Skiing is a business.' And a lot of that had to do with them being surrounded by the best mountain and the best skiers in the country. They saw an opportunity here. People would talk about Squaw or Utah or Crested Butte and we'd just say, 'Shut up, dude, this is Jackson.'"

It started with a 16mm camera and a dream, although swigs—some might even say chugs—of Jack Daniel's certainly played a role. The price tag on the initial package, which included a camera, lens, and tripod, was $6,000. No matter how they rationalized it, $6,000 was an inordinate amount of money for brothers Todd and Steve Jones, Dirk Collins, and Corey Gavitt. None of them had shot film before, let alone produced a movie, which meant the investment didn't stop there. They purchased several more lenses, not that they knew what to do with them or how they worked, and also a thick photography book that would teach the Boys everything they needed to know. The price tag surpassed $10,000.

A former national championship lacrosse player at the University of North Carolina, Corey Gavitt moved to Jackson Hole—or JH as many locals refer to it—in 1992 after he quit his job as an assistant men's basketball coach at the University of Maryland. That didn't quite parallel the Gavitt family's occupational blueprint. Some families have a long tradition of being doctors or lawyers, but the Gavitts were about basketball. Corey's father, Dave, was chief executive officer of the NBA's Boston Celtics when Corey decided that he was moving west, where he became a server at a restaurant in Teton Village, a collection of hotels, condos, shops, and restaurants at the base of Rendezvous Mountain. Dave is well regarded in the basketball world, particularly on the East Coast. He was head coach at Providence College in 1973 when the Friars made their first NCAA Final Four appearance. He was also instrumental in creating the Big East Conference in 1979 and, in 2006, was inducted into the Naismith Memorial Basketball Hall of Fame. Unlike most conversations future ski bums had with their fathers before ditching the comfortable life to the skid life, Dave gave Corey his blessing.

"My dad has always been supportive of my brother and me no matter what we wanted to do," says Corey. "In the end, his thing is do what you love and don't sacrifice that for anything and you'll be happy. So for me it was that I wanted to go west and leave the traditional sports world behind. Having grown up in a gym or on the lacrosse field in Chapel Hill, I wanted to go west and explore the individual sports that the West offers instead of staying in the comfort zone of what I had back east. Once I did, I was addicted, and it was JH for life."

One of the first places he lived was a mobile home along Village Road, the seven-mile spur that links State Highway 26 outside of Jackson with Teton Village. People confuse the town of Jackson with Jackson Hole. Jackson is the county seat and largest town in Teton County, located at the southern edge of the Jackson Hole valley. With the Snake River winding through, Jackson Hole is bordered to the west by the Teton Range, to the east by the Gros Ventre Range, and a series of bluffs and ridges rise above the southern and northern edges of the valley, creating more of a hole than a traditional valley flanked by two ranges. At more than 600 square miles, Jackson Hole is nearly half the size of Rhode Island, where Corey grew up, and its winters can be tooth-achingly cold. One January, the temperature fell to minus forty-six degrees without factoring in the wind chill, thus the need for Jack Daniel's and its belly-warming qualities. Corey lived with roommates in the double-wide trailer, which had holes in the walls that often filled with snow during storms. For heat there was a woodstove, and there'd be hell to pay if someone didn't stoke the fire and keep it going. During the day Corey skied, and at night he wiped tables and filled water glasses in a properly heated restaurant.

One of Corey's co-workers was a dishwasher named Micah Black, who was born into a family of skiers in Whitefish, Montana. A natural athlete who possesses every single quality men envy and women crave, Micah is tall (six foot two), good-looking (longish hair with Marlboro man features), and cool (Mötley Crüe's Tommy Lee and Metallica's Lars Ulrich are among his friends). Other skiers also fit the description, but Micah is why the term "Jackson Rock Star" originated, a title he pontificated with journalist Rob Story in a 2006 *Outside* magazine article.

"Real rock stars don't scare themselves like we do," Micah told Rob. "They don't live with the massive anxiety of a big-mountain descent."

Micah was on skis by age three, and by the time Corey met him in Teton Village, he had made a name for himself as both a skier and snowboarder. Snowboarding's roots date back to the 1920s, but the modern version of the snowboard began to take form by 1980, when Micah was eight. That's when Jake Burton applied P-Tex and other specifications similar to skis to his boards. Snowboarding, though, wasn't well-received by skiers. Just as ski racers dismissed freestyle skiers and the hot-dog scene of the 1970s, skiers viewed snowboarders as punk kids engaged in a silly activity that was a horrible trend that would disappear. Whatever it was, it was deemed an unworthy presence at ski resorts. In 1985, only thirty-nine of six hundred U.S. ski resorts allowed snowboarders, which prompted snowboarders to get creative. In 1979, Mark Anolik stumbled upon a natural hit of snow on Tahoe-Truckee Sanitation Company land in Tahoe City, California. In other words, it was the city dump, and it became the world's first halfpipe. Tahoe locals Bob Klein, Terry Kidwell, and Allen Arnbrister learned of the site and held sessions on what would be called the Tahoe City Pipe.

"They would spend more time shaping it than riding," Klein said of Kidwell and Arnbrister in an article published in *Transworld Snowboarding* magazine. "We were on boards with bungees for bindings, so we were most interested in dropping in and going up the other side. It wasn't really about air."

In 1982, the first official snowboarding event was held in Woodstock, Vermont, but there were only races in the same mold as ski races. The following year at the inaugural world championships at Soda Springs, near Lake Tahoe, a halfpipe event was added. The pipe was basically two lines of chunky snow built into a natural slope. Riders affiliated with Burton, who had spent their time racing on the East Coast, didn't perform well in halfpipe, which was decided between Jake Carpenter and Tom Sims.

"They built the pipe, but it was not good," Sims told *Transworld Snowboarding*. "I was extremely disappointed. Then the Burton (team) threatened to boycott the contest because they felt that halfpipe riding had nothing to do with snowboarding."

Three years later, the world championships were moved to Breckenridge, Colorado, and halfpipes had progressed so much that standard walls were now five feet in height. By then, snowboarders had proven to skiers that they weren't going anywhere. Norm Sayler, owner of Donner Ski Ranch in Truckee, California, was the first resort in the Lake Tahoe area to sell a lift ticket to a snowboarder.

"It was 1980 and a guy with a snowboard came up to my office and asked if he could buy a lift ticket," says Norm. "I told him 'Yeah, go downstairs and buy one.' And he told me that they wouldn't sell him one. So I called up the lift ticket person. They said: 'He's got a snowboard.' And I said, 'He's got $10. Sell him a ticket. I want that money.'"

Micah, though, didn't care about some snowboarder-skiing feud brewing outside of Wyoming. He saw opportunity in both sports. Although he will be remembered as one of the world's best-known big-mountain skiers who starred in more than a dozen Teton Gravity Research films, Micah was a snowboarder in 1992 when he landed his first-ever sponsor, Smith Optics, Inc. Based in Sun Valley, Idaho, and founded by orthodontist and skier Bob Smith, the goggle company was the first to introduce a goggle with a sealed thermal lens and breathable vent foam. Bob skied at Jackson Hole Mountain Resort often in the 1960s and 1970s and was aware of its inherent difficulties. He gladly provided complimentary goggles to those reputed to be the best on what is considered one of America's most challenging mountains.

With the steepest continuous drop in the country and a continental snowpack defined by light and unstable snow, Jackson Hole's entire mountain is avalanche terrain, with nearly two hundred slide paths within the resort's boundaries. Even the lower mountain isn't safe. Following a storm cycle in 1986 when more than five feet fell in less than a week, ski patrolman Tom Raymer died while performing avalanche control in an area called the Moran Faces. It's believed that he was caught in an avalanche that he himself started after detonating a series of explosives that were designed to break loose unstable snow. Self-triggered, man-made avalanches are part of ski patrol protocol during storms in order to make resorts safer, but it is dangerous work since there can be multiple release points within avalanche-prone areas. As he tossed explosives into the slopes, Tom must have felt his positioning was safe and that any unstable snow would release beneath him. Instead, an enormous slab of snow measuring roughly 1,500 feet wide chunked off. The slab swallowed Tom and screamed down the mountain, destroying a mid-mountain lodge along the way. The deposition zone was nearly 4,000 feet below where the avalanche started, covering most of the resort's vertical drop of 4,139 feet.

Smith valued the importance of high-quality gear on such a mountain and knew that Micah would be an ideal athlete to help promote his company. Sponsoring athletes helps with branding, which the American Marketing Association considers an important criterion for businesses. The AMA states that branding isn't just about getting your target market to choose you over the competition; it's about getting potential customers to view your product as the only one that provides a solution to their problem. So theoretically, if you see Micah Black survive a cliff jump—and it looks cool and you want to drop a cliff one day, which can obviously lead to problems for skiers and snowboarders—you will notice what gear he's wearing in addition to how he physically performed the jump. It's just how our brains work. Fortunately for Micah, this theory resulted in free goggles.

At the time, other than an elite group of skiers led by Glen Plake and Scott Schmidt, Winter Olympians were the only ones who could be considered "sponsored, professional skiers." They were given gear from ski companies and oftentimes were provided financial backing from non-endemic sponsors to cover travel costs and living expenses. Smith Optics, though, was one of the first endemic ski companies to sponsor non-Olympic athletes, hooking them up with gear for being nothing more than good skiers and snowboarders. For Olympians, the sales pitch is simple. Win a medal, land sponsors. But the idea that skiers and snowboarders could get free gear for being good—or perhaps just marketable—was a new concept and certainly a breakthrough moment.

"Sick" Rick Armstrong—and now is probably a good time to mention that all Jackson skiers seem to have nicknames, some better than others, obviously—arrived in Jackson around the same time as Micah. Rick attended Fort Lewis College in Durango, Colorado. Afterward, he ski bummed in Montana. Early in the winter of 1989–90, he gave away his car "because it didn't start anyway" and moved south to Jackson. Even if his car did start, it was buried under several feet of snow outside Bozeman and wouldn't emerge until spring. He tossed his keys to an acquaintance and hitchhiked to Jackson with fifty dollars in his pocket.

"All the best skiers were in Jackson, and that's what I wanted to be," says Rick.

Rick got a job at a ski storage company and lived in a two-bedroom place in town. He doesn't recall the exact number of people who lived in the house. Sometimes there were four people, other times there were six, but he did remember that Jason Tattersall moved into a closet. Tattersall, along with Micah, was one of the resort's young, brash, hard-charging skiers. He had a piercing set of eyes, long blond hair, and was presentable enough to land freebies, but Rick was a marketing dream. He had a boyish face, strong jawline, radiant personality, and even a token mole above his mouth similar to Cindy Crawford's. The mole was a distinguishable attribute for Rick, but sending ninety-foot cliffs was even more so. Rick was also persistent.

He wrote letters to companies and told them what he was doing on skis, and he never forgot to include a picture of himself in the envelope. Before long, Rick and Micah were receiving boxes in the mail that were filled with gear. They were already revered for being the mountain's best skiers and enjoyed the traditional perks that come along with that, but they had also just created an additional yet critical element to the evolution of the ski bum. Ski bums are always searching for ways to lower their overhead, and Rick and Micah had just reduced theirs in a way not many recreational, non-Olympian skiers believed was possible in 1990. They had ways to access the mountain, they were being outfitted head to toe with ski equipment, and now it wouldn't take much money for them to live the ultimate dream, which was to get paid to ski.

"I remember you were considered pro when you got free goggles, and honestly we were stoked to get free goggles," says Sick Rick. "I remember having a closet full of goggles and passing them out at parties, and people thought it was the coolest thing in the world. And we thought it was pretty cool, too. We were the happiest people in the world. Skiing every day and getting free goggles . . . what's better than that?"

Free goggles, though, don't pay rent, so it was right back to working menial jobs for Rick and Micah. For Micah, that meant washing dishes at night, which was an agreeable enough situation, but now there was an added distraction. Corey—the newbie skier and server from the East Coast—was in his ear, probing for information that only a select group of skiers in Jackson knew about. He was hearing about people going beyond the resort's boundaries and coming back with stories of limitless stashes of fresh powder. Micah was partially to blame. It wasn't that he was running his mouth. But after it snowed two feet, Micah would walk into the restaurant and have a jack-o'-lantern smile spread across his face. Five hours later, he was still smiling, and Corey knew that nobody could be that happy sliding crates of dishes and silverware through a machine. It was time for Micah to come clean, Corey decided. He pleaded with Micah to take him to these hidden places, but Micah was hesitant. He and Rick were recent additions to an underground ski fraternity called the Jackson Hole Air Force, whose motto was "Swift, Silent, Deep." It basically meant shut the fuck up about what the Jackson Hole Air Force does and where it goes. But if you do open your mouth, use discretion. Micah wasn't sure Corey was worthy because, in addition to the sacredness of the information, ducking ropes was illegal. If they got caught, a Teton County sheriff could issue them citations for trespassing. Even worse, ski patrol could revoke their season pass, which is the equivalent of finding out your best friend is having sex with your little sister. It's depressing news. But Micah, like other Jackson Hole Air Force members before him who had introduced their secrets to others, rationalized his decision in this way. He said to himself, "Well, I know where I'm going and he doesn't. If anybody is going to get caught, it's going to be him."

One night, several months before he would accidentally meet brothers Todd and Steve Jones and form Teton Gravity Research, Corey got his wish. After the restaurant had closed, Micah pulled him aside.

"Do you got a shovel?" asked Micah.

"Yeah," said Corey, who initially wondered if he meant a garden shovel but quickly realized he was talking about an avalanche shovel.

"All right, be at the tram at 8:00 a.m."

"That meant a lot to me because Micah was shown the ropes by the guys before him, guys like Jimmy Zell, Jon Hunt, and Doug Coombs," says Corey. "That's the way it works. Ski towns have their own corporate ladder. You have to pay your dues."

The tram at Jackson Hole Mountain Resort is an iconic symbol in American skiing. The original tram, which opened in 1966, consisted of two red square boxes hanging from thick cables spanning five towers from the summit of Rendezvous Mountain (10,450 feet) to the tram dock terminal in Teton Village (6,311 feet). The new tram, which replaced the old one in 2008, is pretty much the same, though the new cars are rectangular and have a larger capacity. It used to be that skiers could show up after 8:00 a.m. and get first box. Then it got to be that if you arrived early enough and left some equipment in line, you could leave the tram line and keep your place as long as you returned by 8:00 a.m. If you didn't return by 8:00 a.m., your stuff was likely tossed over the railing, effectively putting you at the end of the line. That cut-off time became 7:00 a.m., and then it got to the point where you had to show up as early as 5:00 a.m. on powder days to ensure fresh tracks on one of the early boxes.

In the 1960s, the federal government had an Area Redevelopment Administration that was designed to aid seasonally depressed communities. Jackson residents weren't enthralled that their town had been classified as seasonally depressed, but they didn't have much of an argument, either. Due to its proximity to Yellowstone and Grand Teton national parks, Jackson survived on tourism and ranching, and there isn't much ranching or tourism to be had in January when it's five degrees outside. The Area Redevelopment Administration played an integral role in jump-starting several major ski areas in the American West. Its role in Jackson was contributing about $1 million for the original tram's total cost of

$1.6 million, a major investment for a relatively unknown ski area. Adjusted for inflation, the $1.6 million price tag would have amounted to more than $10 million in 2009. When the new tram replaced the original tram in 2008, Big Red cost roughly $30 million.

Even with the federal assistance, it was a risky financial move for majority owner Paul McCollister, a Stanford University graduate who had purchased land at the bottom of Rendezvous Mountain in 1961. By 1963, he had convinced Alex Morley and Gordon Graham to become investment partners, with Alex being the larger stakeholder of the two. Paul's intention was to make Jackson Hole the focal point of American skiing and a leading candidate for international competitions. To create that reputation, Paul hired Austrian ski legend and 1964 Winter Olympic gold medalist Pepi Stiegler to become the resort's ski school director. With Pepi, Jackson Hole opened in 1965 with minimal success, totaling about 19,000 skier visits that season. (Heavenly Mountain Resort in Lake Tahoe, by comparison has more visits than that on a busy holiday weekend.) One Teton Village shop owner reported no customers on opening day, and Pepi told journalist David Gonzales that the ski school had three lessons that year on December 28, which is typically the busiest time of the year. Jackson Hole had some built-in disadvantages in its quest to become a major player in American skiing. It had a visionary owner, sure, but Paul wasn't very realistic. Jackson was more isolated than Aspen and Vail, which were within five hours of Denver, and to a lesser degree Sun Valley. All three were considered the finest places to ski in the country. Paul, though, figured the tram—the first of its kind in the United States and comparable to those at major European resorts—would sway public opinion and give skiers a tangible reason to overlook the inherent obstacles of traveling to Jackson Hole. Again, he was proven wrong.

After numerous complications involving funding, weather, and construction, the Jackson Hole Aerial Tram opened in 1966, and the resort experienced low visits that season as well. Jackson eventually hosted an international ski race, but events have never generated direct revenue for ski resorts. In fact, they tend to lose money, but owners justify them because they are effective marketing ploys as most events are televised. Owners can advertise to their target audience—people interested in skiing—and add credibility to their resort. Jackson Hole, though, tried to run before it could walk. It had a big mountain and a sleek tram, but Teton Village lacked hotels and restaurants, the type of tourist infrastructure that's required to attract people to the resort and sell lift tickets. Even if thousands of people wanted to visit, they couldn't because there weren't enough hotel rooms. There was a time in the late 1960s when Alex Morley confessed he wasn't sure he could pay the electric bill or his employees because the resort was hemorrhaging money. Many days he was forced to tell patrolmen and instructors that they were off the clock, allowing them to ski on their own.

Jackson Hole, however, soon followed the blueprint of other ski areas, acquiring land at the bottom of the ski area and establishing Teton Village, which would boast hotels and restaurants. To generate even more revenue, Alex and Paul sold residential lots at the base of Teton Village for as low as $10,000, a price that also included a lifetime season ski pass. Paul remained steadfast about bringing international events to the mountain, but he understood the relationship between basic tourist services and a healthy balance sheet. Alex handed over the company to Paul by 1972, citing the continual stress of operating the resort, and then the Kemmerer family bought it in 1992 from Paul, who died in 1999 at the age of eighty-three. Regardless of who owned the resort or how many hotels, shops, and restaurants were in Teton Village, Jackson Hole had a problem no amount of infrastructure could solve: nobody was good enough to ski it.

France's Jean-Claude Killy, who won one of the resort's early international races, told *Sports Illustrated* magazine that "If there is a better ski mountain in the U.S., I haven't skied it." His comment was a great promotional plug, but reading between the lines, he meant "Jackson Hole is a challenging mountain. It's so challenging that nobody else can ski it but me and my friends, who are some of the best skiers in the world."

One of those skiers was Pepi Stiegler, the resort's ski school director, who wondered if the mountain was a little much for the average skier.

"Pepi always told us stories about how great it was in the early days for skiers, but not so great for the owners," says Howie "Hollywood" Henderson. "There was nobody on the mountain. And the people who were on the mountain didn't know how to ski. Him and his Austrian ski school buddies would ride the tram and get fresh tracks for a few hours, then teach a lesson at the bottom for a couple hours, then finish the day with more fresh tracks from the top of the tram. Tourists couldn't go up there. They'd kill themselves."

Across from the Jackson Hole Aerial Tram dock is a parking lot bordered by split log fences. There is a clock tower rising above the dock, with Jackson Hole written in red letters on the side facing the parking lot. To the left are Sublette Ridge and the Hobacks, which mark the resort's southern boundary, wide open expanses with stunted trees that offer thigh-burning descents for nearly 3,000 feet. To the right is Apres Vous Mountain, the part of the resort that first opened to the public in 1965. These sections are nice enough, but directly behind the tram from the parking lot is Rendezvous

Mountain, which rises in typical Teton fashion. It has angled ridges that brush up against a series of cliffs and gullies so steep that trees only grow in pockets. As the trees thin out, the cliffs grow larger, the canyons grow wider, and then the summit cone comes into view. Carved into a final chunk of rock are S 'n' S and Corbet's couloirs, white strips indented into copper-colored cliffs. With such demanding terrain, most of the resort's first descents were made by ski patrollers who had become familiar with the mountain. They were smart enough to respect the chutes and the consequences of skiing them, but they were also curious and accomplished skiers in their own right, which meant they had the perfect ingredients to raise the standard of skiing at Jackson Hole.

In the 1960s, nobody could've imagined skiing Corbet's, which is the less challenging of the two, as it typically requires a twenty-foot jump to enter the couloir. If you make that first turn after the jump and can handle the fifty-degree pitch, you're golden. If not, you're likely to crash into a wall of rock, and then it's up to gravity what happens next. Corbet's Couloir is named after Barry Corbet, a local mountain guide who, after seeing the chute during a tram ride with Paul McCollister in 1963, proclaimed, "People will ski that. It will be a run." When the tram passes the first four metal towers that each rise more than a hundred feet above the ground, a collective chorus of oohs and ahhs rings throughout Big Red as it sways. But as you approach the fifth tower, the terminus of the tram above the powder field known as Rendezvous Bowl, everyone turns to the left and says, "There it is," and points toward Corbet's Couloir. After the tram conductor announces the protocol for the resort and mentions the famous waffles at nearby Corbet's Cabin, the tram stops and the doors slide open.

Skiers and riders scurry off the metal platform, usually into a fierce wind and plumes of blowing snow. Skiers click in, snowboarders strap in. Some disappear over the rise into Rendezvous Bowl. Others escape the maelstrom and walk into Corbet's Cabin, which has ice-encrusted antennas on its roof. Then there are the select few who veer left and follow the signs to Corbet's Couloir. They follow the same line that a teenager ski patroller did in 1967, when he made the first unroped descent into Corbet's. Despite Corbet's place in American ski history, many people aren't aware that Barry Corbet wasn't the first to ski it. That designation belongs to a nineteen-year-old named Lonnie Ball. According to an article in the *London Daily Mail*, Lonnie was standing on the cornice lip, contemplating his next move, when it broke off and sent him into the abyss. He survived and skied out of it. A year later, Hermann Goellner and Tom Leroy performed front flips into Corbet's, feats that were captured on camera and are seen in Roger Brown's and Barry Corbet's legendary film *Ski the Outer Limits*. Once that happened, nothing was considered too dangerous within the boundary lines, nothing except for an even steeper strip of snow fifty yards south of Corbet's.

S 'n' S Couloir is named after ski patrollers John Simms and Charlie Sands. It's narrower and requires a bigger drop and a more precise landing than Corbet's. In the early 1970s, John and Charlie had been eyeing the chute for years before mustering up the courage to leap. One of them, however, was the first, but they made a pact to never mention who was the first to jump. They haven't even told their wives. Their story traveled fast, and The North Face eventually designed an S 'n' S jacket. As poetic as those stories are, none of the characters involved could've known at the time that the most interesting character in the history of Jackson Hole Mountain Resort—and the founder of the Jackson Hole Air Force who raised the bar more than those patrollers—was still just a kid. That kid was Benny Wilson.

Like all good ideas, the Jackson Hole Air Force patches were the result of a serious drinking session. One patch is a light blue triangle, with red skis crossed in front of a white mountain resembling Grand Teton. Gold wings jut out horizontally from where the skis cross. Below the skis are the words "Jackson Hole Air Force" in black stitching, and spread across the bottom of the patch are four black stars. The other patch, which has become more famous, is a black diamond with white stars in each corner. A white skull in the middle is surrounded by the motto "Swift, Silent, Deep" in gold letters. Underneath the word *Deep* is a red banner stretching across the length of the patch with "1st Tracks OB" stitched in gold. Below that and above the bottommost star is the acronym "JHAF." Great thought and massive amounts of alcohol were put into the simple designs—at least that's how the story goes by those who can remember.

The year was 1984, and the Teton Range was getting pounded by storms rolling off the Pacific Ocean and merging with cold air pushing south from Canada. There was too much snow for the resort to open. To temper the anticipation of the ensuing powder days ahead, Benny, Howie, and other resident ski bums waited out the storm in the Bear Claw Café, located in the bottom floor of a Teton Village building. While others watched ski movies, drank beer, and rattled off the parts of the mountain they'd ski whenever the storm ended, Benny sat on a bar stool and sketched drawings on a napkin. Tower 3 Chute, Alta Chutes, Rendezvous Bowl, Moran Faces, Hobacks . . . it was going to be heaven on earth. But for now it was about gelande quaffing and Benny's sketches. Gelande quaffing is when the bartender—or anybody else—slides mugs of beer across the bar. As the beer flies off the edge of the bar, the person who ordered it is required to catch the mug in mid-

air and chug it. It was a village pastime during the rise of the
Jackson Hole Air Force. The activity was resurrected in 2009,
when there was an official Gelande Quaffing Championship
in the Village Café, which replaced the old Bear Claw Café
and remains a popular ski bum haunt. (There is a rumor that
Benny and Howie were on the winning team in 2009, but I
could never obtain official results.) When the winter storm
broke, everyone got fresh tracks, but Benny remembered to
take his napkins and get patches printed. He immediately
handed one to Howie, his best buddy, and said, "Here, put
this on your jacket."

"What is this?" asked Howie.

"We need to have a name for us. We're the Jackson Hole
Air Force."

Us, as Benny was referring to with Howie, was a group of
skiers who had earned a reputation around the village for
partying, cutting-edge skiing, and colorful antics. The group
grew to include but was not limited to Jimmy Zell, Jon and
Rick Hunt, Tom Bartlett, Kevin Brazell, and the venerable
Doug Coombs. It was typical ski bum behavior for the decade, but Benny and his friends were doing it on the steepest,
most avalanche-prone mountain in the country. Benny, for
his part, had already made a name for himself in Jackson Hole
because of his father, Colby, who started the family's pattern
of rebelliousness.

In the summer of 1966, Colby brought his family from
Cleveland, Ohio, to Wyoming for vacation. When they finished
riding the tram up Rendezvous Mountain, which made them
some of the first people to ride the tram, the Wilson family
dined at a Teton Village cafeteria. Colby disappeared during
the meal, then came back to announce that he had taken out
an option on a nearby piece of property. The property became
Hostel X, a two-story wooden boarding house that opened

that winter and charged a flat fee of ten dollars per room, regardless the number of people. If you were serious about skiing, Hostel X was the place to stay. Posters, photographs, and articles, many of which highlight JHAF skiers, plastered the hotel's walls, making it a Jackson Hole ski museum. When movie premieres by ski filmmakers such as Warren Miller and Dick Barrymore came to town, they were shown in Hostel X's basement. There was also plenty of ping-pong and drunken conversation. The Hostel X atmosphere was a stark contrast to what Paul McCollister and Alex Morley had envisioned. They wanted a European-style village, with shops and restaurants on the first floor and residential units on the second floor. They wanted sophistication, not barbarism. They wanted tranquility, not chaos. Colby Wilson, though, didn't want what Paul wanted. He never embraced Paul's frugality or controlling nature, wrote David Gonzales in his book *Jackson Hole: On A Grand Scale*.

"Paul McCollister refused to pave the roads or the parking lot," Mike Wilson, Benny's brother, told David. "There was a hole in the main road, probably two or three feet deep. So my dad decided to do something about it. One morning, Paul came driving down the road, headed for his office, and there was a tree planted in the hole. It was a good-sized tree, too, five or six feet tall."

Soaking up such outlandish behavior by his father and patrons of the Hostel X was Benny, a child who quickly adapted to life in the mountains. The Hostel X was the Wilson family house, and their backyard was Rendezvous Mountain. By the time he was a teenager, Benny was an accomplished ski racer, though he preferred aerials more than gates. Pepi Stiegler and his Austrian buddies put on aerial displays and held ski races on the lower mountain to the delight of the town's skiing youth. To Benny and other local kids, speed and air were king and what defined a great skier. Pepi Stiegler was the fastest and sent the biggest airs, therefore he was the best.

Benny joined the Marines after high school, but he eventually returned to Jackson. One day, Benny and his friends were drinking in the Mangy Moose Saloon, another institution in the village, and decided to take their skis and climb the roof of the nearby Inn at Jackson Hole hotel. It then became a tradition to ski the hotel's roof. On the tram, people weren't quite sure what to make of Benny, a dark-haired fellow who wore jean jackets and rocked out to music inside his head. He has pale green eyes, thick, dark eyebrows, and a set of cheekbones that appear to be permanently woolen, a result, I decided, of so much smiling over the years that they just decided it was easier to stay flexed. He also dressed in costumes to disguise himself from ski patrol when he skied in closed areas. One December, he wore a Santa Claus outfit and ignored every closed sign on the mountain. Two ski patrolmen confronted him, but one of them told the other, "You can't be mean to Santa, can you?" I never really got the true story of why he left the Marines, but my best guess is Benny doesn't follow orders and he tends to break rules, which aren't characteristics of Marines. Whatever the reason, it didn't seem to affect him upon his return to the Tetons, and he eventually applied a modified version of the Marine phrase "Swift, Silent, Deadly" to describe his group of ski buddies. He had skied every inch of Rendezvous Mountain by 1979, when a blond-haired, medical school dropout named Howie Henderson arrived from Michigan. Howie, whose father gave him his blessing to become a ski bum as long as he did it in Jackson Hole, got a job at the Alpenhof Lodge, which was run by Pepi Stiegler's son, whom Howie's father had gotten to know during Henderson family ski vacations.

"There is this modern-day ski bum that works in order to

ski, but when I got to Jackson, ski bums didn't work," says Howie. "Of course everybody needs to work to get by and have a little money, but ski bums never had season passes or bought lift tickets because they knew the lift operators. Ski bums didn't work to ski in the beginning. They bartered, not because they wanted to, but because they had to. They didn't have the types of jobs you have now in ski towns. If you were a server in a restaurant, you gave free food to lift operators. If you were a bartender, you gave free drinks to lift operators and servers in restaurants. If you were a lift operator, you turned your head when the bartender and server approached the lift. That was the original ski bum."

Howie, who grew up skiing at Boyne Mountain in Michigan, was introduced to Benny through Wade McKoy and Bob Woodall, two local photographers who almost single-handedly documented the progression of skiing at Jackson Hole during the 1970s, '80s, and '90s. If there was a ski shot of Jackson Hole in a magazine in those decades, it was probably taken by Wade and Bob, who started Focus Productions in 1976 and became the resort's unofficial marketing department. They connected with the tram operators and bartered to get first boxes with the patrollers to ensure perfect morning light and fresh powder shots.

"When we first started shooting skiing, it was pretty obvious right off the bat that you needed to work with the best skiers on the hill," Wade is quoted as saying in *Swift, Silent, Deep*, a documentary released in 2009 about the Jackson Hole Air Force. "With Howard shooting them already with Teton Video, we went along with Howard. And these guys were the best skiers on the hill."

Ski patroller Rick "Frosty" Frost moved to Jackson from Connecticut in 1977 because he saw photos in *Powder* magazine that were shot by Wade and Bob. The amount of snow, the abundant sunshine, the blue skies, the steep mountains—Frosty never believed there could be such a combination. Frosty, though, isn't the only skier to have moved to Jackson because of Wade's and Bob's photography.

"Those shots had a pretty big effect on me," says Frosty. "But when I got to town in the fall, I looked up at the ski runs and wasn't very impressed. I realized I was looking at Snow King (a small resort behind the town of Jackson), so I drove out to the village, saw the big mountain and thought 'This is a little more like it.' But when I got my job on the ski patrol and stood on top of some of the chutes, I was in over my head. I liked the pictures and the thought of skiing those chutes when I was in my bed in Connecticut a lot more than I did when I was standing on top of them. It took me a while to get up to speed at this resort."

Benny launched a cliff one day, and the white contrails of snow behind his skis were backdropped by a cobalt-blue sky. The jump was photographed by Wade, and the picture was published on the cover of *Powder* magazine the following winter. Focus Productions compensated him with a five-dollar check, which Benny still has. It's one of the few pieces of evidence that proves Benny was a professional skier, but that doesn't mean he wasn't one of the best.

"I really admired the way he jumped," says Howie. "He could really catch some air, and he tried to do it with style. He also skied very fast, and he did it with style. That was the biggest thing with us early Jackson Hole Air Force guys. Style was very important to us because style defined the guys we admired. We looked up to Pepi Stiegler, the Austrians who were ex–World Cup racers. They were the best skiers of our day. They'd go ski crazy couloirs, launch the most stylish jumps, and then enjoy a bottle of wine and eat escargot. They'd make a hundred of the best turns you've ever seen, skiing from top to bottom, never stopping, and then have a hundred chicks hitting on them at the bottom of the hill. We felt we weren't worthy. I don't think Benny admired much about my skiing, but I think he admired my midwestern brashness. I think the reason why Benny and I got along so well is that we both felt the same way about things. He was fresh out of the Marine Corps, and we didn't take shit from anybody. We complemented each other really well."

The precise origin of the name "Jackson Hole Air Force" is still up for debate, mostly because there is some truth behind Benny's prophecy: "If you can remember skiing in the eighties, you probably weren't here." By most accounts, however, it derived from hot-dog contests in the 1970s. Benny and other future JHAF members were still in high school at the time, and the contests always included disciplines such as aerials and ballet-style skiing. The judges determined that the Jackson Hole skiers were never very precise in their turns, but they always had the biggest airs, to which ski patroller Lonnie Ball, the first to ski Corbet's Couloir, started throwing around the name the Jackson Hole Air Force. It became a lighthearted way to describe Jackson skiers, but it never really became a hallmark name until the 1980s when Benny, Howie, and others started pushing the boundaries, both from a skiing and philosophical standpoint. Howie's father bought two businesses in the village, one of which became the Bear Claw Café and the other Teton Video. As manager of the video store, Howie had access to a camera that he used to film Benny instructing his customers during ski school lessons, as well as ski races on the weekend. He also used it to film his buddies. Howie and Benny would work together on making a program called *Eye Over the Tetons*. It mostly showed video clips of ski instruction and races, but they'd bridge the gaps between them with a more exciting brand of skiing.

"Benny never thought much of the quality of our films, but they were pretty good considering the video camera we were using and the amount of drugs we were on half the time," says Howie. "When you're jumping off thirty-five-foot cliffs, as long as you get it on camera, people are going to like it. Benny ... he's the king of the one-liners. He always said, 'When the camera comes out, the IQ goes down.'"

With Howie as the color commentator, Benny and others were shown flying off cliffs, ripping powder lines, and making tight, precise turns in challenging terrain. When the film switched from beginners to experts, it announced: "Now starring ... the Jackson Hole Air Force." Howie took the footage and aired the tapes at night in the Bear Claw Café. Ski bums and tourists would huddle in the basement bar, glued to the television. Nobody really got worked up over the ski instruction shots, but the bar exploded with the footage of JHAF skiers. It was clear what people wanted to see from skiing films—action. Then in 1982, a photo series of Jackson skiers taken by Wade and Bob was published in *Powder* magazine. The caption associated with the photos made a reference to the Jackson Hole Air Force.

"Between the *Powder* pictures, *Eye Over the Tetons,* and Benny just being his flamboyant self, we became the Jackson Hole Air Force," says Howie. "Ski patrollers started telling us that we're taking too much air ... that we're poking around in the trees too much ... that we're skiing in closed areas. It became too much for them."

The Jackson Hole Air Force's objective was simple. It wanted to ski powder. Not after snowstorms. All the time. It wanted to ski powder more than do aerials, moguls, and freestyle tricks. It became an obsession. At first, that meant searching for powder within the resort's boundaries. When all the fresh snow had been skied off on established runs, they'd launch off huge cliffs because, as Benny said, "If you jump the biggest cliffs, you're guaranteed to have first tracks and a soft landing at the bottom because you're the only one to have done it." If ski patrol planted a closed sign above the Hobacks, Howie and Benny skied past it. If ski patrol closed the chutes near Thunder Saddle chair, Howie and Benny "opened" them.

"Fuck ski patrol," says Howie. "That's how a lot of us air force guys felt. What do you mean I can't ski past that closed sign? Why are the Hobacks closed? Don't tell me I can't do something. I can do anything I want to do, and ski patrol can't stop me. I will drink them under the table, and I ski faster than them. I used to go right up to their faces and tell them where I'd been poaching, and then I would tell them, 'Why don't you come ski with me, you fucking pussy?' That's the way I talked to them because, let's face it, ski patrol are just cops, and we know why people become cops. They want to feel like they are in charge and have authority. They only became ski patrol so they could ski powder, and now they're going to tell me when I can ski powder? I came from a liberal college town and believed in three things: Vietnam was bullshit, rules are meant to be broken, and don't trust anybody over thirty. I ran onto the field drunk at the Big House at Michigan football games, with security all around, and am I going to follow orders from ski patrol when I can ski three feet of fresh blower powder? Not a chance."

For the most part, ski patrol left the Jackson Hole Air Force alone in the early 1980s. Benny, Howie, and their ski buddies were nuisances, of course, but they weren't endangering other skiers. In fact, many of the air force and ski patrol members were friends. That all changed in 1986 when Tom Raymer died in the avalanche. Reeling from a public relations nightmare, resort management put immense pressure on the ski patrol to become more diligent in avalanche-prone areas and to strictly enforce closure signs. Ski patrol made it clear that the mountain doesn't open—and that means any part of the mountain—until it says so.

"And we had a response for that as well," says Howie.

In the 1980s, skiing off the established runs was considered daring and dangerous. The terrain wasn't groomed. There were unmarked obstacles. A skier could easily become lost in bad weather. The JHAF decided that off-piste skiing increased one's likelihood for fresh tracks, therefore it was smart. And they had a point. If an accident occurred, ski patrol was available to rescue an injured skier. But skiing beyond the resort's boundaries—purposely ducking the orange ropes—was viewed as suicidal. Even if a skier was an experienced hiker, the landscape changes in winter. Familiarity in August doesn't mean familiarity in January. At resorts, cliffs and other hazards are marked. Beyond the boundary, nothing is marked, and there aren't any trail maps. When the angle of a slope reaches a particular steepness, it's impossible to know if the cliff in front of you is a hundred feet high or ten feet high. Also, there weren't cell phones in the 1980s and for most of the 1990s as well. If something happened, you had to be self-sufficient until Teton County Search and Rescue found you—and that's assuming you stayed alive. Worst of all, avalanches were not only possible but likely. Teton County often leads the country in avalanche fatalities. These days, people who go into the backcountry carry rescue beacons, which assist in locating an avalanche victim (assuming the victim is also wearing a beacon and has it turned on). They have probes to find someone's precise location, and they have shovels to dig victims out of debris. There are hundreds of avalanche safety courses offered throughout the year, most using a nationally approved curriculum for instruction. There are also up-to-the-minute avalanche reports for backcountry users in mountainous areas. In the 1980s, snow science was a relatively new field, and typically ski patrol were the skiers educating themselves on avalanches.

Benny Wilson and Howie Henderson didn't care. Just beyond the boundaries at Jackson Hole Mountain Resort is the holy grail of North American skiing—Granite Canyon, Rock Springs Canyon, Cody Bowl, Cody Peak, No Name Peak. The JHAF pioneered them all. When ski patrollers went to perform avalanche control in certain areas, they didn't like seeing ski tracks going past the orange boundary ropes and then see on the other side of the canyon more ski tracks tattooing blankets of fresh snow. Admittedly, their first reaction was one of jealousy (several ski patrol members were JHAF guys on their days off), but their attention quickly turned to the security of their jobs. They didn't worry about the abilities of JHAF members, who were expert skiers capable of navigating through hazardous terrain. And if they weren't capable, they knowingly broke the rules and were aware of the potentially lethal consequences. However, it was one thing for experienced skiers to tackle fifty-degree couloirs and powder fields on copper-tinted mountain faces for 2,000 feet, but it's quite another for a three-day-a-year skier from Missouri to enter that terrain. Ski patrol didn't want tourists seeing JHAF tracks and following them into the wilderness. It was a legitimate concern, and it became a dilemma.

Ski patrol had grown close to the JHAF over the years, and what they were about to do was jeopardize that friendship. They couldn't risk losing their jobs and they didn't want to be responsible for an innocent tourist's death because he followed Howie's tracks into Rock Springs Bowl. It was time to lay down the law. It was decided that if ski patrol caught anyone skiing out of bounds, that person could get a tongue lashing but most likely they'd get their ski pass pulled, particularly if they were JHAF. Ski patrol teamed up with the Teton County Sheriff's Department, and skiers were issued citations for trespassing if they were caught skiing out of bounds. Since the resort is surrounded by public land, most notably Grand Teton National Park, skiers wanted to know why they were receiving tickets for being on public land. It was a legitimate gripe—though it got a little tricky because they accessed that public land via a private company's lease agreement with the government—but regardless, it was happening.

To stay one step ahead of ski patrol and the sheriff's department, air force members would stash clothing and other gear on various parts of the mountain. They'd wear a red jacket when they ducked the rope near the top of the tram, and then change into a black jacket upon reentering the resort and returning to the tram. The JHAF established a backcountry cave that proved to be an effective hideout, but ski patrol discovered the cave and destroyed it by tossing avalanche explosives near it. Ski patrol used walkie-talkies to communicate, then the JHAF bought walkie-talkies to listen to what was being said about them. It was total cops and robbers, cowboys and Indians.

"That's where Benny's 'Swift, Silent, Deep' came into it," says Howie. "We had to be swift to get past the ropes and disappear, but we had to be fast getting back into the boundary because ski patrol was watching us. That's why we stashed different-colored jackets in the forest. We had to be silent because we didn't want anybody knowing where we're going. Not only could we get in trouble, but why would we tell people where they can find five feet of blower powder and ruin it for the rest of us? Fuck that. I am not even against jabbing one of my friends with my ski pole if he gets in my way, who knows how I would treat some tourist. And then it was all about deep powder. We're talking miles of limitless, bottomless powder. We're talking a couple dozen of us having powder days all day, every day for years. It was a very special time."

As much the JHAF fought to protect the information they were gathering—access points to canyons and mountains and avalanche awareness—they respected great skiing. Just as the ski patrol watched the JHAF, the JHAF watched other skiers. Benny and Howie weren't naïve enough to think that they were the best skiers on the mountain. New waves of skiers arrived every winter. Had Benny ignored everyone, he never would've noticed a guy in a dark-colored jacket in 1986 who is remembered as one of the best skiers ever—not in the country but in the world. Benny knew the mountain better than anybody else, and he absolutely blistered the slopes when he put his mind to it. There were only a few people faster than him, and he knew who they were. Most of the time, it was fellow Jackson local Jon Hunt, a candidate for the U.S. Ski Team. On an established run that's groomed—and if Benny wasn't determined to point his tips—it was possible somebody he didn't know could slide past him. But this guy wearing the dark-colored jacket was off-piste, where the terrain is uneven, so Benny decided to ramp it up a little.

Who was this guy? He had the tightest, most precise turns Benny had ever seen, and the increased speed didn't seem to affect him. Benny increased his speed even more. It's okay to get passed by Jon Hunt—one of the fastest skiers in the country—but it's not okay to get dusted by a complete stranger. Benny always had another gear, but his form usually suffered when he entered it. This guy's form seemed, though, to improve as he went faster. And he was so fluid. Benny was breathing heavy now, but this guy purred along like a kitten, giving Benny the impression that he could've continued skiing like this for 10,000 feet.

Benny and Howie had developed a system of handing out JHAF patches to those who were deemed worthy. Sometimes they gave them out to someone who hooked up with a hot chick or someone who scored a high-quality sack of marijuana, but most of the time they kept it to skiing-related credentials. Whether or not Benny learned that person's name was of little concern since he figured he'd learn it eventually. But this guy in the dark-colored jacket had just passed Benny and was flying down the hill in perfect balance. Benny obviously would give him a patch, but when he finally caught up to him—when they were both standing in the tram line—he forgot about the patch and introduced himself. The patch would come, to be sure, but who the hell was this guy with the goofy teeth, the vibrant smile, and the smoothest turns he had ever seen? Turns out he was a recent college graduate of Montana State University who went by the name of Doug Coombs.

"When you saw Dougie ski, it stopped the clock," says Howie. "He was so relaxed, so confident, so stylish, making all these turns. You'd never think something could be that beautiful, for that long, but that was Dougie on the mountain. It almost blinded you, like a spotlight was on him when he was skiing. He stopped all of us JHAF guys in our tracks, and nobody could keep us from skiing. But we'd just stand there and watch him ski. He skied better than Stein Erickson and Pep Stiegler, but he skied just like them. He was skiing the steepest lines we had ever seen, but then he could throw a big, styly cliff jump, stick the landing, and immediately start making those Dougie turns. Basically, there was your life before you saw Dougie ski and after you saw Dougie ski."

By the end of the 1980s, Benny and Howie wanted the JHAF to remain relevant and that meant the crew needed new blood. But if Doug Coombs was an example of the types of skiers being produced in this country, it wouldn't be long before they gravitated to Jackson. And it also wouldn't be long before Benny and Howie were no longer leading the charge. In accepting this realization, they also knew that not every skier would value what they had valued—and they eventually came to grips with that as well.

"Benny and I talked one day and we agreed that if we want this to continue, there has to be a new generation," says Howie. "If something happens to one of us air force guys in the backcountry, we can only rely on ourselves. It's like a family, but all of a sudden there are these new kids coming in and doing crazy shit, and it's not like we are going to be out there to help them forever. We could take them in, let them hang around us and teach them stuff, but there was a limit to what we could do. We were starting to have families, kids, whatever. Dougie came from a racing background, but Rick and Micah didn't buy into the racing mystique like we did, and they were part of the new generation. They were these flamboyant freeskiers who couldn't ski worth a shit, but they were skiing steep lines and throwing big airs. We started out handing patches to them. So we had two generations coming together, but they were two generations with two different mindsets. Promoting ourselves verbally was not our way. We were old school. We didn't understand it, but we noticed that the new schoolers were all about it. In our day, if you thought you were good and ran your mouth, we'd look at the results of the weekly Bartender's Cup races. 'Oh, you say you're good, Sick Rick, but I don't see your name on here. Why don't you do a little better next week in the race and then come and talk to me?' And if Rick's name still wasn't on the results list, I'd tell him to shut the fuck up and then punch him in the mouth. But we entered the age of promotion. Sick Rick, people would say, 'Well, he was good enough. He was good looking enough. He tells people he is a good skier, and then they believe him and give him free stuff.' Suddenly, Rick is skiing in Antarctica with Warren Miller, and he's getting free skis. Everyone's talking about Sick Rick and if I saw him do this and that, did I see him ski this line or that line. Yeah, I've seen the guy fucking ski for years. He'll jump off any cliff out there, but he skis like shit. Good friend of mine, though."

When I rode the resort's Bridger Gondola with Rick one morning, he confirmed what Howie had told me. Rick admitted that he and the others who arrived during that era like Jason Tattersall and Micah Black were wide-eyed kids who admired the JHAF. He said his best day of skiing wasn't when sponsors started giving him gear or paying for travel costs; it was when he was given his JHAF patch by Benny.

"Those guys, the Doug Coombses, the Jon Hunts, the Howie Hendersons, the Benny Wilsons, those guys showed all of us youngsters how bad at skiing we really were. We thought we were good before we got here, and then we'd see those guys ski. It took all of my strength and energy to keep up with them. I'd take one look at Jon Hunt make a beautiful arcing turn at sixty miles per hour on hard pack and think 'Yeah, I'm never gonna be able to ski like that.' But I could send ninety-foot cliffs, so I did that."

By the late 1990s, there wasn't just Wade McKoy and Bob Woodall documenting those cliff jumps. Wade and Bob always said that to get the best shots you need to hang with the best skiers on the mountain. But what happens when the best skiers are the ones getting the best shots?

"Basically, once the Jones brothers showed up, everything changed," says Howie.

Kodak Courage

Anybody who sits at a coffee shop complaining about how there's a new stoplight in their ski town should go spend a month in Cleveland and get a little attitude adjustment.

—Filmmaker DICK BARRYMORE, who directed *Last of the Ski Bums*, in *Powder* magazine

It doesn't look like much, just a metal grated staircase rising above picnic tables outside the Village Café to the second floor of a gray building. There are blue railings along the staircase, which takes a sharp left and ends at a glass door with a blue handle spanning its width. There are three decals midway up the door, the largest one being a Teton Gravity Research sticker that's starting to fade and show the effects of a decade's worth of ski and snowboard edges. I pull open the door and walk into a foyer. There is another door on the other side, and an article in a wooden frame that's nailed to a white wall. It was written by Jackson-based ski journalist Tom Bie. The story was published in the local newspaper on August 21, 1996, shortly before the release of Teton Gravity Research's first film *The Continuum*. Tom details the timeline of how co-founders Corey Gavitt, brothers Todd and Steve Jones, and Dirk Collins went from being skids and ski bums to, well, skids and ski bums who produced a film about skids who were skiers and snowboarders. The Boys didn't have to look far for movie talent. Steve, Todd, and Dirk were not only co-founders of the company, they were sponsored skiers whose friends were sponsored skiers and snowboarders. As a result, they had the fortune of forming relationships with some of the world's best.

Five years earlier, Doug Coombs won the inaugural World Extreme Skiing Championships in Valdez, Alaska. Jackson Hole Air Force skiers secured the next two spots in the standings, and also most of the top ten. The best part of the contest, in the eyes of the JHAF, was that there were no rules. No ski patrol, no orange boundary signs, no resort management. Skiers came from around the world to be judged by Scot Schmidt and Glen Plake, but Jackson skiers were most prepared for the fifty-degree hanging snowfields and shark- tooth spines of the Chugach Range. Squaw Valley and Crested Butte skiers were technical and talented, but they hadn't been exposed to the same sustained pitches and objective hazards that they would've been had they been skiing, say, Granite Canyon and Cody Peak.

The Chugach Range is peppered with 4,000-foot faces that—in 1991—had never been skied. Just getting down was enough for most skiers. There was trash talking before the competition, which was advertised in *Powder* magazine, but it stopped once the turns started. If a skier fell in this terrain, death was conceivable, if not certain. The Jackson Hole Air Force demolished the competition and won resort bragging rights. Coombs, though, wasn't able to defend his title the following year because he had convinced fellow JHAF skier Jon Hunt to participate. Before the competition even started, Jackson skiers conceded defeat and told event organizers to just give first place to Jon, who didn't disappoint. He used a combination of Doug's style and his incomparable speed and applied it to the steepest slopes outside the European Alps that were being skied at the time. The width of skis was much thinner then, and the only way to ski that steep of terrain was to make controlled jump turns. Jon didn't ski like that. He never deviated from his downhill racing style, ripping race turns on forty-degree faces and leaving jaws dropped. He showed what was possible on skis—speed and style in the backcountry.

"Every skier you see today was influenced by Dougie Coombs and Jon Hunt, whether they know it or not," says Howie Henderson. "Anybody who's on ESPN in the X Games or in a TGR film, their skiing was influenced by those guys."

Doug won the contest again in 1993 and by then the terms *freeskiing* and *extreme skiing* were coined to describe the style of skiing in Valdez. Doug and his wife, Emily, teamed with Alaska West Air Taxi, which provided access to the peaks, and started Valdez Heli-Ski Guides, the first guiding operation in the Chugach. There are now more than a half dozen guide operators in the area, but Valdez Heli-Ski Guides was the first, and for good reason. Coombs and his friends were responsible for many of the range's first descents. No other skiers in the world knew the mountains better than them. They operated out of the Tsaina Lodge, where "Sick" Rick Armstrong worked as a dishwasher. Within three years, Coombs had a crew of twelve guides, either Jackson Hole Air Forcers or trusted confidantes. The Tsaina Lodge was Village Café North. Even Benny Wilson made it to Valdez. Everyone seemed to be there, including brothers Todd and Steve Jones and Alaska native Dirk Collins. It was the wildest skiing on earth, and, best of all, there wasn't a Teton County Sheriff waiting for them at the bottom.

Ski and snowboard film companies started showing up in Valdez to document the progression of the sports, but only a few produced annual movies. There was Warren Miller, but he was strictly skiing. Standard Films and Mack Dawg

Productions, which started in the 1980s and 1990s, were strictly snowboarding. No film companies provided a crossover of the two sports—none until Steve, Todd, and Dirk formed Teton Gravity Research.

"I was going back and forth between Jackson and going to school in Montana, but I really wanted to go to Alaska and check out the Valdez scene," says Todd. "So I dropped out of college in 1991 and sold all my stuff and went up there and got on with a commercial fishing company. We made some money in the summer, and then we hooked up with Coombs and started guiding for him. We'd fish into the fall and then get ready for the winter. After a couple cycles of that, the TGR seed was planted, but it was more than that. It was more than watching other film companies and saying 'Why don't we just get some cameras and film ourselves?'

"We knew how the industry worked because we were sponsored, but we thought the system was broken. Warren Miller [Films], they'd have a deal with Rossignol and skiers would show up to a film shoot and wear Rossignol stuff for a week. Then they'd want us to ski this low angle stuff at the bottom of the mountain and didn't want anything to do with the high angle stuff at the top of the mountain, the type of stuff we were skiing. So we'd shoot with Warren Miller, make a hundred turns on an intermediate slope, then watch ourselves in the film and be unhappy with the final product. Rossignol would be happy because it was promoting their product. Warren Miller was happy because he was promoting his product. And resorts were happy because their product was being promoted, but we felt the athletes were the real product.

"We thought companies should be sponsoring athletes and film companies based on agreements and contracts. So we set out to fix the system by promoting the athletes and the direction of the sport instead of just promoting resorts and film companies, not knowing if we would be successful or not, but we felt it was the right thing to do. We wanted to shift the paradigm and, from a business standpoint, get these athletes acknowledged because skiers were doing amazing things.

"We also wanted to show that these athletes were people, showcase their skills on and off the mountain, show more of the lifestyle. I don't know when exactly those things merged. Valdez was a great example of that combination of skiing and lifestyle, but you weren't seeing much of that in films. Looking back, it doesn't seem like it should have been that hard. Yeah, we didn't know how to use an editing system. We had been around cameras before because we had been filmed, but we didn't know how to operate them. But the most important thing was we knew the lines we could film because we were already skiing them, and we knew the characters because they were our friends. Now we just needed the cameras showing Sick Rick and Doug Coombs shredding the shit out of the mountain."

Once through the second door by the newspaper article, there is a lobby. The floor creaks upon entry, and to the right is a wooden bar in a semi-circle shape with an assortment of maps and pamphlets scattered on the surface. On the other side of the bar is a white refrigerator with a collage of stickers on the side, mostly TGR decals but also a red, oval-shaped Session beer decal. There is a thirteen-inch television on top of the fridge. Next to the fridge is a large poster of Bob Marley, whose music is featured in the company's early films. On the same wall is a shrine of TGR athletes, either magazine cover shots or full-page advertisements in wooden frames. A white track lighting system hangs above the shrine. Farther to the left are more rooms and another collage of photographs. There is a poster of snowboarder Jeremy Jones, considered the best big mountain rider in the world and the younger brother of Todd and Steve, on Cody Peak, a panorama shot of the Jackson Hole Aerial Tram backdropped by a layer of fog in the valley, and another poster of Cody Peak.

The rooms are fronted by an open area sliced into separate work areas by a partition board. Wires and cords dangle from the ceiling. In the vicinity are bindings, videos, bookcases, dressers, even a surfboard, none of it in any particular order. There is a guy with a serious case of bed head sitting on a chair and sipping soup from a bowl. A brown pit bull walks around with little regard for people's established position, knocking into someone's knees if they impede his progress. Todd's husky goes from room to room, lying next to whichever chair suits him best. Josh Nielsen, TGR's supervising producer—a title whose meaning he is unsure of—is engaged in an animated discussion with a skier in a green jacket about backcountry filming locations in a canyon inside Grand Teton National Park.

Back toward the entrance is an unlit Jack Daniel's neon sign above the lobby door and an aging six-ounce Coca-Cola can that leans against a speaker mounted to the wall. Opposite that wall is another wall that connects with an upstairs loft, which is reached by a rickety, non-OSHA-approved wooden ladder. A twenty-five-cent lemonade sign hangs down from the loft's wooden floor, visible from the lobby. Below the lemonade sign and attached to the ground floor is a cubby, like one would have in elementary school. Instead of books and backpacks, however, its compartments are filled with helmets, shoes, and gloves. In the room adjacent to the cubby is another Jack Daniel's sign, this one with "Our Benevolent Sponsor" written underneath it.

Corey is in the room nearest this Jack Daniel's sign and is sitting at a table with another guy. Both are staring at a

computer and nodding their heads. A strip of navy blue carpet curls past the room where Corey is seated and ends at
a locker room being populated by the general public. I am
not sure of the access point to the locker room, but nobody
seems to mind the intermingling because it's been snowing
for the past five days.

Everyone's happy. It's mid-February. Storms are hammering
parts of the United States and Europe. Steve Jones is filming
in Europe, and Josh Nielsen will be in Italy later this week to
film a crew of professional skiers and snowboarders. More
rooms splinter off from the hallway with navy carpet—one
of them is the Boys' main office, another is the editing room,
another is a storage room. In the summer, when the filming
has ended, the editing room is ground zero. While the rest
of the Jackson is mountain biking, climbing, and getting a
tan in July, every member of the TGR staff spends twelve to
sixteen hours every day cooped up inside this square room
putting the finishing touches on the year's upcoming film. At
the moment, the Boys' main office is littered with snowboard
bags and boxes stacked with film. The snowboard bags are
empty and the compartment flaps spread open, the weight
of the zippers folding them toward the floor.

Corey and Todd are headed to Alaska the next day to film
another crew of professional skiers and snowboarders, but they
need to pack. Todd, Corey, and Josh will speak with me today,
I am assured—and they eventually do but in ill-defined time
slots—though they seem rather agitated at me poking around
the office. More than likely, however, the tension level is height-
ened because the success of next year's film hinges on this storm
cycle, because who knows when it might snow again.

"It's February and we don't have any shots of Sage yet,"
says Josh about Sage Cattabriga-Alosa, who has been named
Powder magazine's skier of the year. "We can't come back
empty-handed. We can't get skunked. Everything about

the film industry is difficult because so much of it involves things that are out of your control, and usually it's weather related."

Josh grew up in Vancouver, Washington, and became a ski film addict while attending college in Montana. Wearing a red jacket, Josh has a mop of blond hair, dark-colored eyebrows, and is pacing around the office asking "Does anybody know where a 240 lens is?" before scurrying in another direction. There is no sign of Dirk Collins, who recently parted ways with TGR—under amicable terms, I was told—and started another company. The duties of the three remaining co-founders have shifted a bit. All of them film, but they manage specific departments. Corey is responsible for developing, marketing, and branding the TGR clothing and apparel line. Todd focuses on the technology side, which includes producing television shows and commercials, and he also manages the company's new media arm. TGR's official Web site, tetongravity.com, enjoys more than 5 million page views per month, 300,000 unique users per month, 100,000 video streams per month, and has nearly 30,000 registered users. Steve, meanwhile, handles sponsors, the critical element of TGR's business model, but more on that later.

"We all have our specific areas, but we all chip in where needed," says Corey. "It wouldn't work any other way."

Although there can be fifteen people wearing ski and snowboard boots in the office at any given time, the number of total employees fluctuates depending on the season and economic climate. When I wrote a story about Jackson Hole in 2005, there were more than a dozen paid employees. When I returned in 2009 to report on this book, I counted on two hands the number of employees, but there was still a music editor (Dustin Handley), a supervising producer (Josh) who also works as a cinematographer, and a media relations worker.

I think the guy sipping soup also has a title, but it might be "unpaid intern," which TGR employs several of.

Rewind to 1995, when there was Todd, Steve, Corey, and Dirk living in a one-bedroom condo that served as TGR's headquarters. They outfitted the place with a fax machine, a telephone, and cupboards filled with Top Ramen. When the phone rang one evening, everyone looked at each other and collectively asked, "Who could be calling? Does anybody know we exist?" Micah Black wanted to find out. He picked up the phone and said "Hello," to which Dirk yelled at him and said "No, no, Teton Gravity Research."

To generate sponsor support, all of them would drive around the American West trying to secure funding for their upcoming films. They slept in their vehicles most of the time because there wasn't any money in the budget for hotel rooms. As more national and lucrative sponsors climbed on board, the Boys quit their other jobs, because for the first time in seven years, they could pay themselves a salary. If the company made money, it went to its films and the few employees it had.

Up until the turn of the twenty-first century, Dirk, Todd and Steve's exploits as fishermen in Alaska funded the initial camera package and the early films, while Corey continued to work menial resort town jobs and build the company's brand with a slick logo and apparel line. For its first film in 1996, the company's marketing assistant was none other than Sick Rick Armstrong, who starred in TGR's early films with Dirk, Todd, and Steve. While fishing and skiing in Alaska was a major influence on TGR, a chance meeting with Corey provided an element of destiny in Steve, Todd, and Dirk's endeavor. Micah's initiation of Corey in the Jackson Hole backcountry that day in the early 1990s went well, and they began hanging out together since. One night at a party, Corey was standing next to Micah, beer in hand, and asked, "Is that Steve Jones over there?"

"Yeah, but how do you know Steve?" Micah replied.

Corey grew up in Providence, Rhode Island. His family had a second home in Cape Cod, Massachusetts, where the Jones brothers grew up. Their younger brother, Jeremy, learned to snowboard on golf courses. During Gavitt family trips to Cape Cod, Corey, Todd, and Steve became friends, but they grew apart after high school. Corey had heard something about the Jones brothers going west and becoming professional skiers or being fisherman in Alaska. Corey, though, had no idea that they were in Jackson until that night. Teton Gravity Research might have been born on the slopes of the Chugach Range, but it was conceived at a Jackson house party.

If *The Continuum* was released in 2009 and not 1996, Teton Gravity Research might have crumbled. By today's standards, the sound quality was weak, the filming was grainy, and the editing process was suspect. The music didn't mesh well with the action clips, and the editors didn't even bother implementing voice-overs during segments, opting instead to plug in face-to-face interviews between clips with athletes who likely had puffed a succession of bong hits.

Even sponsors weren't well taken care of. After the opening clip of a massive avalanche cascading over the cliffs of Rendezvous Mountain into Tensleep Bowl, there is a cartoon showing a spaceship landing on the moon. When it lands, an astronaut exits the spaceship and steps onto the moon. His boots display the shoe company Simple on the soles of both feet. In a slight breeze, companies start to appear on a fluttering flag. Ride, *Telluride Outside* magazine, *Powder* magazine, Smith Optics, Life-Link International, Croakies, *Rage* magazine, and Jackson Hole Mountain Resort. In all, nine sponsors, three of which were regional companies, received a combined thirty-two seconds of airtime. It was as if a bunch of amateurs were making their first film, which was exactly the case. In 2009, treating sponsors like that would be suicide, but it wasn't 2009. It was 1996. At the Walk Festival Hall in Teton Village, the Boys figured maybe a few hundred people would show up to see *The Continuum*. Instead, it was standing room only and then some.

"There was a line of cars coming down the village road, like that movie *Field of Dreams—*If you build it, they'll come," Dirk told author David Gonzalez.

A new era in ski and snowboard films had begun, but Jackson Hole's response to *The Continuum* illuminated a new trend. Mack Dawg Productions, a snowboarding-specific film company, got started in 1988 when Mike McEntire traveled out of his car, figuring out ways to scrounge up money for his next film. Standard Films, another snowboard film company, was founded by Mike Hatchett in 1991. A year later, Matchstick Productions released its first skiing-specific film. Those companies were the ones showing up in Chugach Range in the early 1990s, and TGR continued the proliferation of action sports film companies. Every company holds an annual film premier. It creates buzz for the film and starts to give sponsors a return on their investment. But compared to the demographic at Warren Miller film premiers in Jackson Hole, the Boys noticed a younger, more animated crowd at the TGR premiere. Other film companies noticed it as well, and it was evident that skiers and snowboarders were searching for something other than Warren Miller, whose personal story is intertwined with the history of skiing.

After serving in the Navy, Warren attended the University of Southern California. In November of 1946, it snowed in the

San Gabriel Mountains outside Los Angeles. He went skiing the first weekend it was possible, and on Monday he dropped out of USC. At the age of twenty-six, he convinced his friend Ward Baker to move with him to Sun Valley, Idaho. Warren owned a trailer, and they towed it behind their vehicle and lived in the resort's parking lot. If they got short on food, they shot rabbits. To gain access to the mountain, they handed a six pack of beer to the lift operators "and we had season passes from then on," Miller told cinematographer and former TGR supervising producer Jon "JK" Klaczkiewicz in the documentary *Swift, Silent, Deep*. "[At that time, Sun Valley and the other resorts] were filled in by young people, World War II veterans, Tenth Mountain [Division] guys, people who didn't like living in the city. For me, it was my first memory of traversing across that hill. I really believe it was my first taste of freedom. I went as fast as my courage allowed. It's just what I wanted to do."

In their spare time, Warren and Ward filmed each other skiing with an 8mm camera and then used the footage to critique one another's technique. Warren began filming other skiers and, in 1946, created Warren Miller Entertainment. He released his first feature-length film in 1950 titled *Deep and Light*, and every year for the next six decades his movies have been played in packed theaters. From New York City to San Francisco, skiers and non-skiers were attracted to his witty humor and distinct voice, not to mention the superb athletes and photography. His bloopers were legendary. He'd return to Southern California, where residents are marginal skiers, and film people getting off chairlifts and falling. Except for the occasional film by Roger Brown, Dick Barrymore, or Greg Stump—who was the first to start documenting the progression of the sport in the 1980s by filming Glen Plake and Scot Schmidt—Warren Miller's films were annual community events and staples of winter. Growing up in Salt Lake City during the 1980s and later while attending college in the early 1990s, Brett Barratt, a lawyer who lives in Lake Tahoe, never viewed December snowflakes as signs of winter. He used a different calendar.

"Winter started when the new Warren Miller movie came out," says Brett.

Warren Miller ran the company exclusively until he sold it in 1989 to his son, Kurt, who then sold the company in the early 2000s to Time Inc. Time has taken advantage of the Warren Miller name and still produces an annual film, though his fingerprints are no longer part of the finished product. Now in his eighties, Warren no longer narrates the films. Starting in 2005, sound bites from his previous films were woven into the narration, a contrived attempt at duplicating the creativity and authenticity of Warren's films. However, the Warren Miller brand still attracts a crowd. The movie tour stops at more than two hundred cities nationwide and several locations outside North America. Mountain Sports Media estimates that the film premieres attract more than a million viewers annually. It was reported in a 1999 *Outside* magazine article that Warren Miller Entertainment's annual profits were roughly $13 million.

When TGR's 2007 film, *Lost and Found*, premiered on the south shore of Lake Tahoe, it was held at Vex Nightclub inside Harrah's Casino. There were drink specials and DJs spinning hip-hop beats as well as topless dancers shaking it in cages. When Matchstick Productions released *Seven Sunny Days* in Whistler, British Columbia, 3,000 people showed up, and the film premiere turned into an all-night party for twenty-somethings. I watched *Seven Sunny Days* in a nightclub in an industrial area of San Francisco. The film was a prelude to a concert that night. Scott Gaffney, a cinematographer for

Matchstick Productions who was in San Francisco that night, said that other film companies can't compete with Warren Miller's tour popularity, but the torch has been passed in the eyes of the skiers and snowboarders who have moved on from his style of films; however, Warren's imprint on the action sports film industry is undeniable.

"Warren Miller films started it all for many filmmakers and skiers," says Scott. "For a huge segment of the skiing population, Warren Miller films are all they really know, particularly for the true recreational weekend warrior. Those people associated Warren Miller premieres with autumn and imminent snow and got to the premieres like drones. That's not meant to be condescending—it's just what they do. I really haven't seen Warren Miller movies for the past decade. They stopped speaking to me a while ago. Or, more appropriately, I grew out of them. For another crowd—particularly the more serious skier who wants to see the most progressive lines and moves of the year, and watch those moments over and over within their homes—the Warren Miller movies don't hold up anymore. While no company matches Warren Miller's tour draw, companies like Matchstick Productions sell far more films, because that's more what the hardcore, younger skier is looking for. That viewer doesn't want just entertainment— he or she wants to study the movie, learn new tricks, mimic what their heroes do, and see the limits of what is possible on skis."

In other words, they want to see ski porn.

Dick Barrymore's *Last of the Ski Bums* was released in 1967, the year America was learning that a ski bum culture existed. Ski racing was the most popular form of skiing, but just as Vietnam draft-dodgers moved over international borders, skiers moved beyond the ski boundaries and adopted a different mentality. Dick's main character in the film is Ron Funk, who has never had a job and prefers wine, women, and song. He lives out of a Volkswagen bus in the European Alps and finds two other ski bums to join him on his journey. They travel down the powder road, skiing and scraping their way through France, Italy, and Austria. They also visit Monte Carlo and win enough money gambling to buy a Porsche and live high on the hog until the money evaporates. The film was funded by the French tourism board, which gave Dick $15,000 to make a promo film for French resorts. Dick told Ron and the other two skiers that he couldn't pay them anything, but their expenses would be covered. They barely had enough money to reach the Geneva airport at the end of the trip.

"It just reeks of timeless soul," Corey Gavitt told *Powder* magazine. "It's the blueprint for every one of us that have gone down that path, and not just from a filmmaker's standpoint. He captures the vibe of spending a season in the Alps on a shoestring, where happiness isn't about being cool or rich or skiing the burliest line in Chamonix, it's about living it. And while everything else in the ski industry has changed in the past forty years, that feeling hasn't."

Roger Brown's *Ski the Outer Limits* in the late 1960s used a similar vein as *Last of the Ski Bums*. It was about skiing, of course, but there was a philosophy behind it. When front flips are performed into Corbet's Couloir and the narrator states, "What was impossible yesterday is today's absolute limit, tomorrow's commonplace. Today, this is the limit." That turned out be a statement that defines today's film industry. In the 1970s, Greg Stump's *Blizzard of AAHHH's* was released, featuring Scot Schmidt and Glen Plake, and it too combined stunning ski footage with strong narration and careful editing. These films are considered classics, ahead of their time but timeless. *The Continuum* was TGR's first attempt at a new style of ski film, one that attempted to include a storyline but not at the expense of sick ski footage. They provided some insight into the minds of skiers, but mostly it was about powder turns on big mountains and hucking cliffs. Whatever the combination, it sold more than 8,000 copies within a year, but TGR's next film, *Harvest,* was the breakthrough project. *The Continuum* was mostly shot in Wyoming and Idaho, and to a lesser degree Alaska and New Zealand. In those last two locations, they were under time constraints and the weather wasn't cooperative. The cameramen experienced cloudy skies, minimal snow conditions, and bad light.

"We pretty much used everything we shot in those days," says Corey. "With the budget we were operating on back then, film was gold. We didn't have the budget we have today and the money to overshoot. Now, we can shoot three hundred hours of film and condense it into a forty-five-minute film. Back then, if we shot it, it was probably making it in."

As he leans back in his chair and laughs, Corey, with a dip of chaw in his mouth, goes on to say, "That's probably how I made it in there."

Corey got a short segment in *Harvest,* which was filmed in a similar amount of locations as *The Continuum,* but with the weather gods' cooperation. As a result, TGR put together what was considered the finest big mountain ski and snowboard footage from Chamonix, Alaska, Italy, and Greenland. Every time they landed at a new airport, it was snowing. The next morning, the skies were cobalt blue.

"If that doesn't happen, if the skies don't open up for us, who knows if we would've made it, because we were really struggling to get by," says Corey.

The athletes started to change a bit as well. *The Continuum* featured skiers and snowboarders almost exclusively from Jackson Hole, but *Harvest* showcased several non-Jackson athletes such as former U.S. Ski Team member Jeremy Nobis and Utah freeskier Brant Moles, who won the 1995 World Extremes in Valdez. Jeremy, at one point in the film, shreds a 2,000-foot line on a fifty-degree face in Alaska's Chugach Range. In previous years, skiers would make fifty turns down that face. Jeremy made six. TGR was documenting the evolution of skiing. In the late 1990s, the collection of talent was expanding, the jumps were bigger, and the tricks more advanced. Jackson Hole legends such as snowboarder Julie Zell, Sick Rick Armstrong, Micah Black, and Doug Coombs figured they'd always have a role in TGR's future films.

"I like working with those guys, because I know them and trust them in the mountains," Julie told journalist Tom Bie for an article published on MountainZone.com. "It's also easier for me to work with people who know what I can do. Sometimes people just assume because I'm a snowboarder that I'm going to huck myself off anything. And I don't. That's not just what I do."

Julie miscalculated. TGR might not assume that she's going to huck herself off anything, but many of the companies that sponsor athletes and film companies expect them to. Each year TGR produces a new film, the soundtrack and picture clarity have increased in quality, the number of sponsors has increased, and the number of Jackson athletes has decreased. In the 2007 release, *The Tangerine Dream*, Micah Black is the only member from the JHAF who is featured. The lineup consists of the hottest skiers on the planet, including Peter and Michael Olenick from Colorado and Utah's Sage Cattabriga-Alosa. Sick Rick isn't in TGR's films anymore. Neither is Julie Zell, Kevin Brazell, Tommy Moe, or Doug Coombs, who died in a 2006 skiing accident in La Grave, France.

"I still get some benefits from being a skier, but nothing like the guys are getting today," says Sick Rick, who's now in his forties and working as a real estate agent in Jackson. "What skiers now bring to the table is insane. They face death or serious injury all the time. Let's just say they aren't stoked about just getting free goggles."

Before *The Tangerine Dream* begins, there is a lengthy preview for a TGR surfing movie. Rip Curl, a major sponsor of TGR, enjoys more than a half dozen product placements in the preview. I didn't see a single other company's logo or apparel. When the camera is interviewing one surfer wearing a brown shirt, the camera cuts him off about mid-chest, though the Rip Curl logo across the middle of the chest remains. After the surf movie preview and before the ski movie begins, there are four minutes of sponsorship plugs, national outdoor companies ranging from The North Face to Burton. The only sponsors remaining from *The Continuum* are Jackson Hole Mountain Resort and *Powder* magazine.

"You see a difference between all the filmmakers between their films now and when they first started," says Jon Klaczkiewicz, who was a supervising producer and cinematographer at TGR before quitting and producing documentary-style films without funding from corporate sponsors. "It doesn't matter if it's TGR or Matchstick Productions. Take Scott Gaffney [now at Matchstick], his *Walls of Freedom* film is so soulful and one of my favorite films ever. It was so beautiful because it was back when people were shooting their friends. As you bring in more corporate sponsorships and endemic sponsors, those sponsors have an agenda and expectations. You're not going out to shoot your friends anymore."

JK and I chat over frosty mugs of Sierra Nevada Pale Ale on a picnic table outside the Village Café. It's late in the afternoon, and the chairlifts have stopped turning. I finished my interviews with Todd, Corey, and Josh earlier that afternoon. Todd noticed JK sitting at the wooden table on his way to the parking lot.

"Are you guys headed to Alaska?" JK asks Todd, who's walking down the staircase from the TGR office.

"Yep," answers Todd, his snowboard bag slung over his shoulder.

"Have fun," says JK.

I am certain that Todd gave our table a second glance. Perhaps he had recognized that the writer from Lake Tahoe is now speaking with a former TGR employee, but maybe it was my paranoia. JK didn't pick up on the glance, but he did say there was bad blood when he left.

"I honestly felt like my creativity was being inhibited by sponsorship relationships," says JK, who left in 2003 after three years with the company. "The Boys were pretty pissed because they kind of took me in. I wanted to do something different. I thought there was a lot more potential to tell stories. At the end of the day, what's a ski film supposed to do? It's supposed to inspire people and stoke people. I didn't feel that was happening the way I wanted to any longer at TGR."

At TGR, JK was an executive producer and managed a crew of athletes. He filmed around the world, enjoying the pleasures of all-expenses-paid trips to Europe and Asia. The novelty soon wore off. If he returned from trips and his best shots weren't of a particular athlete, he'd get a tongue lashing from one of the Boys. That meant he'd have more pressure to get a shot of that particular athlete on the next trip. At first, JK simply figured the Boys' creative juices were the culprit and that they were envisioning beefing up their options and having segments of certain athletes in locations around the world. The more images they had of that athlete, the better the film would end up being, JK thought, but he was mistaken. He didn't know it at the time, but before he even left for the Alps it was decided which athletes were going to be in the film. In addition, it had already been decided how often that athlete would appear in the film and for how long. He obviously knew the athletes he was working with were sponsored skiers and snowboarders, but he didn't know that he was being used as a pawn to execute a detailed, meticulous business contract that was signed before the first snowflake fell.

When Sage Cattabriga-Alosa flashes on the screen at the beginning of *The Tangerine Dream* and slays it on the mountain in the opening segment, his main sponsors, like Rossignol and The North Face, paid lots of money to ensure that happened. Sage throws flips off cliffs and rips powder turns on Alaska faces. That's why Rossignol and The North Face sponsor him. He's awesome. And that's why Rossignol and The North Face are the sponsors revealed before the film started, but their involvement is more than just writing a check to TGR and telling them "Good luck. Hopefully you get some shots of Sage while you're in Alaska." It might have started out that way, but it's not a coincidence that the technical quality of TGR's films has improved each year. By attracting national sponsors with deeper pockets, it's equated to better equipment, better locations being shot, better athletes being shot, and a stable salary for the Boys.

"In order to survive, TGR has created a machine that has to be subsidized, and in order to get subsidized, you have to sell out," says JK. "You can't make money selling a few thousand films. Nothing in the film hasn't already been negotiated and worked out beforehand. Sponsors want to know how much their logo will be on the screen. They want to know how many of their athletes will occupy the first three segments of the film. They want to know how many seconds their logos will be shown and how many minutes their athletes will be shown. If they pay more money, the sponsors are guaranteed the first three segments and more product placement, more time on screen, and so on. Those are the conversations before the winter. Once it's been agreed upon, it's written in a contract and signed by both parties. TGR then goes out that winter and honors the contract."

When he realized this was the arrangement, JK's mood soured, but he bit his lip because he had one of the more coveted jobs in the winter sports industry. He grew up a weekend skier from Colorado Springs, went to the University of Colorado at Boulder, and moved to Jackson after meeting Sick Rick Armstrong at an industry convention in Las Vegas. He had already known about Jackson Hole and its reputation. He also knew about the Jones brothers and was a fan of their films. It was his dream to work for TGR, helping produce films and managing the most talented skiers and snowboarders on earth. He became a sponsored skier himself, landing segments in TGR films. Eventually, though, he couldn't rationalize it anymore, and he aimed his moral compass a different direction.

"Sponsors started taking the creative energy away from the film. You'd just go shoot their athletes in beautiful places and convince yourself that you've made a great film, but all you've done is make a collaboration of talented athletes. And they are talented, but the soul of the film has been lost. It's no longer shooting your friends. It's ski porn. I got into skiing because it was for the love of the game, and I got into filming because I wanted to film with my friends and hand out high fives with everyone. But my job was reduced to 'Did I get an A+ shot of so- and-so?' If I did, I did a good job that day. If I didn't, I did a bad job. When you're getting subsidized by sponsors, everything changes, and it changes for the athletes. I think they started doing this for the love of the game and somewhere along the way it turned into a job. If there wasn't a camera, I don't think many of these athletes would be doing the things you see on camera. But their lives depend on getting the shot. If they don't get the shot—and they continue to

not get the shot because they don't want to or for whatever
other reason—then they won't have any sponsors. If I didn't
come back with an A+ shot—and if I continued to not get an
A+ shot of a certain athlete—I wouldn't have had a job."

When JK left TGR, he helped produce a film titled *Reverence: The Kent Kreitler Movie*. Kent starred in TGR's early films
and is one of the more accomplished big mountain skiers in
the country. JK didn't receive major sponsorship funding for
the film, and his latest film, *Swift, Silent, Deep*, was financed by
credit cards and other money he scraped together.

"If I had wanted to bring in corporate sponsors, I could've
ended up with more sleep, a lot less fights with my wife, and
got the movie finished in half the time," says JK.

"I really wish I had talked to you before speaking with the
Boys," I told JK after finishing our second round of beers.

"It doesn't matter. They wouldn't have talked about it anyway," says JK.

In a series of follow-up questions, I asked Corey to comment on what JK told me on that cold February afternoon.
He would not.

"On the sponsorship thing, I'm not going to get into answering those specific questions," Corey explained in an e-mail.
"Reason being that those relationships—and the guts of our
business—are off-limits. I hope you can understand. Stick to
the cool vibes of the local scene in Jackson, bro. That's what
people want to hear about."

This goes beyond Jackson Hole. If the current structure of
the film industry can influence ski bums to alter their values
for money—the very thing that they've vowed not to care about
in their pursuit of freedom—exactly how much money is being exchanged here? The dilemma used to be at what point
is a ski bum a professional skier? Now it's at what point is a
professional skier no longer a ski bum?

The superpipe at Buttermilk Mountain is felt long before it's skied. It's late January outside Aspen, Colorado, and the local busses are packed. Packed like a Tokyo subway. Faces pressed against the windows. Arms contorted like a game of Twister. Before the doors can close, everyone must take a collective breath. When the doors open in the parking lot, bodies exhale and are tossed out of the aisles into the mud and gravel. Only a few people could see it, me being one of them, but there was a massive white glow on the drive in from Aspen's Rubey Park bus station. It lit up the Rocky Mountain sky. Once at the Buttermilk parking lot, the contrast between inky night sky and massive white glow had been blurred. The sky was only white, and I was in the middle of the glow.

Two rows of fourteen stadium lights, similar in wattage to those at a minor league baseball stadium, hovered several stories above a halfpipe that is much larger than the Tahoe City pipe in the 1970s. Its walls are twenty-two feet in height, with blue lines crisscrossing the jowls and deck, but nobody seems interested in the details. Thousands of people have congregated at the bottom of the pipe. Most are no older than twenty-one, and they have more alcohol flowing through their bodies than the rest of Aspen combined. Of the two dozen arrests this week, nearly all were alcohol related, and more than half of those involved underage drinking. Aspen police and event security aren't very effective, but they are overmatched. Over the course of four days, more than 72,000 people will have passed through the gates adjacent to the Buttermilk parking lot. At thirty, I feel like I'm back in high school. The kids wear hoodies, baggy jeans, and jewelry poking through holes in their faces and ears. They hold iPhones above the crowd and, with outstretched arms, take pictures and document the melee. Girls climb on the backs of boys and wrap their legs around their shoulders. Rising above the

throng of people, with long hair flowing beneath their bean-
ies, they unzip their jackets and tease the male-dominated
crowd. They lift up their shirts and act like they will show
their breasts, but it's snowing and twenty-eight degrees. Their
naked skin can't handle the conditions—or the fear of ending up on YouTube is too great—so they zip up their jackets
and scream, apologetically, "Sorry, boys." Suddenly they have
orange juice bottles that don't contain an ounce of vitamin
C in both fists and are taking swigs out of them.

The bus was bad; this is unbearable. I decide to climb the
stairs on the left side of the halfpipe; they lead to an icy thirty-
degree slope that gets me so close to the action that when skiers soar above the pipe's lip, ice crystals spray off their edges,
float in the air, and coat my face. It is three minutes until the
start of the men's skier superpipe finals, and my escape plan
proves ineffective. As the crush of people squeezes out pimple-
faced teenagers, they start to climb the stairs, and I get an
uneasy feeling that these pierced hyenas will eat me alive if I
don't hold my ground. Within two minutes, there are as many
people on the sides of the superpipe as at the bottom of it. It's
like a mosh pit at a Pantera concert. Instead of two-hundred-
pound behemoths pushing me around, it's featherweight high
school chemistry students and twenty-something Brazilian
girls. I didn't mind the girls so much, though I was forced to
kick steps in the ice and anchor myself to the slope, but I was
outdueled by the pretty girls from Brazil. Their bronze skin
was mesmerizing in the whiteness of the Colorado winter.
They also took swigs from juice bottles filled with rum and
pressed against me until their shoes were in my steps. Their
smiles were seductive, and I was now anchorless. There was
nowhere else to go. The sides of the superpipe were packed
five people deep on either side. I was, more or less, on the
first line and incapable of moving more than a few inches

in either direction. The arches in my feet were beginning to cramp. I began to lean on a middle-aged woman whose eyes were as large as deviled eggs. Somebody was more frightened than I was.

Welcome to the 2009 Winter X Games.

It's showtime. The snow stops falling. The Brazilian girls no longer smile at me. A thirteen-year-old skier wearing a purple, one-piece outfit and a fourteen-year-old skier in a bumblebee yellow jacket drop in at the top of the superpipe. One follows the other, and they dazzle the screaming, drunken crowd with a succession of aerial tricks and maneuvers, flying above the lip, spinning like a kite on a breezy day at the beach. Just as colorful, too. In 1990, they would've been the best skiers on the planet. But these are just the forerunners, a pair of up-and-coming skiers who test out the pipe one final time before the competition starts, the appetizer before the main course. I am here, in a parade of kids who still tuck condoms in their wallets, to see Simon Dumont, a twenty-one-year-old from Maine who is considered one of the top superpipe skiers in the world. His main rival is Tanner Hall, who's won a record seven gold medals at the Winter X Games. Nobody else has a chance in the minds of everyone here, though France's Xavier Bertoni pulls an upset and beats them both.

Now in its fourteenth year, the Winter X Games hypes both Simon and Tanner, almost to a fault. Earlier in the week, more than a dozen skiers were attempting to qualify for eight spots in tonight's finals. At the top of the superpipe is a black inflatable starting gate structure with "Winter X Games" and other sponsors printed in blue lettering. There's also a large-screen television/scoreboard that introduces the skier currently in the superpipe. No matter which skier was attempting to qualify a few nights ago, the name and face on the screen was either Tanner or Simon. Tanner is a bit of a renegade, having earned a reputation as an accomplished skier and shit disturber. He has blond hair, blond eyelashes, and a thin blond mustache, but he talks like he's from Harlem and dresses like he's a rastaman from Jamaica. At the age of twenty-one, he was arrested in Vail for accosting an employee at a bar following a podium finish at the U.S. Open, a freeskiing event held the week before the Winter X Games. One year at the Winter X Games, he complained that one judge didn't like him and that's why he lost to Canadian Charles Gagnier in slopestyle. Slopestyle is a competition that incorporates all the elements of a terrain park—rails, jumps, and boxes. As in superpipe, slopestyle is subjective because judges crown winners, and it's one of the reasons some purists prefer ski racing. The fastest person down the hill wins. It's the definition of objective. But Tanner got the ski racing world's panties in a bunch when he told a magazine that Bode Miller and other ski racers don't deserve multi-million dollar contracts because they only have to ski down "one icy-ass run."

Tanner was raised in Kalispell, Montana, and became one of the top mogul skiers in the country as a youth. He didn't like the structure of mogul skiing and gravitated toward freeskiing. He filmed with TGR as a teenager in 1999 and soon was dominating the competition circuit. Just as they no longer film their buddies skiing, film companies no longer show just one type of skiing. One reason is that skiing and snowboarding has expanded to include big mountain, racing, and terrain park. The other reason is that in recent years because of competitions such as the Winter X Games and smaller circuits like the Dew Tour and the Swatch Ticket to Ride Tour, sponsors expect their skiers and riders to be the total package. The better-known companies such as TGR and Matchstick Productions used to exclusively show mostly big mountain clips, but now it's a combination of big mountain and terrain park, including superpipe. There are also plenty of urban terrain park features in films such as launching off parking garages and sliding handrails on staircases, to which Daron Rahlves, one of the world's top downhill ski racers, responded to Tanner's disparaging remarks and categorized freeskiing in this way: "He's young, and he's in his own little freeskiing world," Rahlves told *Ski Racing* magazine. "To me, I think it's great the way they expand the sport, and it's something the industry must pay attention to. But jumping on rails is more like rollerblades. To me, it's not skiing. . . . These guys are impressive and they work hard to accomplish these tricks, but it's the same thing over and over again. I posed a challenge to Tanner. I said I'll hook you up with some downhill boards and you come up to Val Gardena or Kitzbuhel. And just make it to the bottom."

Tanner never accepted his challenge, but there was little reason to. It's like two millionaires comparing the size of their dicks and how many yachts they have because, well, they are two millionaires. Although it's difficult to compute the exact salaries because winter sports athletes are paid by sponsors who never release that information, industry experts believe that top ski racers Bode Miller and Daron Rahlves earn more than seven figures, according to *Ski Racing* magazine. Tanner Hall and Simon Dumont aren't children of the poor, either. Michael Spencer, Simon's agent, said the top freeskiers in the world are probably making more than $500,000 per year. There's a big drop-off after that, Michael explained to me in an Aspen coffee shop the week of the X Games. But since he represents one of the top freeskiers in the world, when he throws out the $500,000 a year figure, I deduce he is referring to Simon. I am not, however, concerned with salaries. I want to know if Simon will let me shadow him for the week of the Winter X Games, and I ask Michael this question before the event. I tell him I am writing a book about ski bums and want to profile a professional skier.

"I have a little problem with your request because Simon is not a ski bum . . . he's a professional athlete," Michael tersely tells me over the phone.

"I understand, and that's why I want to profile him for my book, to understand the differences between ski bums and professional skiers."

Michael seems satisfied with my response, and he assures me that Simon won't have a problem with my request. I am satisfied as well because I am running out of options. There were only a few days left before the event and Tom Yaps, Tanner Hall's agent, had already turned me down. I contacted Tom a month before calling Michael. CR Johnson, another one of the world's top freeskiers, is a good friend of Tanner's and is from Truckee, near Lake Tahoe. I contacted CR and asked him if he could set me up with Tanner. CR told me to get a hold of Tom because every media request goes through Tom, who tells Tanner which ones are worth accepting. I asked Tom if Tanner would mind me following him the week of the X Games for a book I am writing. After a back- and-forth process where Tom talked with Tanner, and then Tom talked with me, Tom told me it's not possible.

"He's just really focused right now. He's got a chance to do something really special and he doesn't want any distractions," says Tom. "But he's got no problem doing maybe one interview sometime during the week."

A month before the Winter X Games, Tanner was arrested on drug charges in Boulder after police spotted a group of people doing ski stunts near a high school. The officers approached the crowd and smelled marijuana. Tanner claimed it was his, and he pleaded guilty to possession of drug paraphernalia. After the arrest, his mother told the Boulder-based *Colorado*

Daily newspaper, "He's not the only athlete out there who smokes marijuana. They all do it."

I called Tom during the Winter X Games to arrange an interview to talk about the arrest and other topics, but he never returned my call. In eight years of working as a reporter, I have been snubbed by two people. One was a high school girls soccer coach who was upset that her team didn't score, to which my response was "It's soccer, nobody scores." The other snub was when Sterling Sharpe, a former NFL All-Pro wide receiver, walked past me at a celebrity golf tournament in Lake Tahoe. I held out my hand to introduce myself, and Sterling slapped it away. How is it possible that I've been able to get quotes from Jerry Rice, the best receiver in NFL history, when no other reporter could at the same celebrity golf event, but I get turned down by a pot-smoking skier from Montana? That's okay. I will talk with Simon, Tanner's rival.

Simon stands me up all week. When he wasn't competing, he ignored me. Early in the week, Michael told me he was focused on the competition but promised that he would sit down with me. Anytime we're both available, he was either napping or making sponsorship appearances. If it was 11:00 a.m., he was napping. If it was 3:00 p.m., he was napping. If it was 6:00 p.m., he was napping. If he was between naps, he was leaving to sign autographs at Quiksilver or Billabong or a ski shop with Salomon equipment. Simon has so many sponsors that I began to lose track. He started out with Oakley and Salomon as a high school student in Bethel, Maine. In 2003 he signed with Red Bull, a non-endemic sponsor. And within the last few years, he's become the first American skier to sign major sponsorship deals with Toyota and Target. The red-and-white one-piece ski suit he wears for the superpipe competition looks like the Target logo, and it's not unintentional. His entire body is a billboard. His helmet has Oakley and Red Bull paraphernalia, and when he takes his skis off after each superpipe run, he never forgets to flash them toward the camera to make sure his sponsors get their plug.

"It's kind of taken on a life of its own now," says Michael. "Simon Dumont is a brand in skiing. He is synonymous with Salomon and Oakley; those were the companies that jump-started his career. It's more than putting a decal on a ski or a helmet. And when you bring in sponsors like Target and Toyota, it's great for the industry. It makes skiing seem more credible. It's like 'Hey, Toyota sponsors Simon Dumont and cares about skiing.' Maybe that will have an effect when someone buys a car. So we foster all of our relationships. They all chip in, some more than others, and provide him a living, split the travel costs, etcetera. Skiing is his nine-to-five job. In the winters, it's competition after competition. In the spring, he does some filming. [In 2008, Matchstick Productions cameramen filmed Simon airing thirty-five feet off a quarterpipe, a world record. The tower measuring the height of the jump was sponsored by Red Bull.] In the summers, he's training in New Zealand and working out until the fall, and then he's back here getting ready for the winter. In between, he does all sorts of media ops where he takes care of his sponsors and fulfills his obligations for them."

No wonder he can't talk to me. Not only is he busy, he's selective about who he is busy with. If I can't talk with him, I will talk to his fans. Abby Widman and Allie Alter are fifteen years old and from Ohio. They saw Simon on ESPN last year in the Winter X Games and traveled to Aspen this year to see him in person. They aren't alone. With more than 300 media credentials issued, more than 72,000 fans at the event, and with ESPN's and ABC's eight live telecasts of various events averaging 900,000 viewers worldwide, the Winter X Games can reach everyone. The giggly girls from

Ohio pleaded with their parents to allow them to skip school for the week and attend the Winter X Games. When they heard their parents had a conference in Aspen, they felt it was destiny. After superpipe qualifying, where Simon finished fifth, they waited for him at the bottom of the superpipe. They yelled his name and he walked over and asked if they wanted to take a picture with him. They melted. He wrapped an arm around each girl and smiled for the camera. Afterward, they jumped and screamed, causing people to turn in their direction. Simon, meanwhile, turned the other direction and signed autographs. Abby and Allie looked into their camera and screamed again.

"I can't believe it," Abby shouts.

They walked through the venue toward the bus stop, passing by advertisement banners from companies such as Nature Valley, Taco Bell, Red Bull, Jeep, Aspen/Snowmass, Zippo, Oakley, Edge. Edge shaving gel is an interesting sponsor since nobody at the Winter X Games seems old enough to shave, but I guess Abby and Allie shave their legs. I walk with them past the Buttermilk parking lot to a bus stop along Highway 82. As they wait on a curb, snow begins to fall.

"We came all the way from Ohio to see Simon," says Abby, who admits she has fifty pictures of Simon on her wall at home. "He's so cute and so amazing. I want to marry him."

"Do you ski?" I ask.

"Not really, but this is the greatest day of my life," Abby says. "We're coming back tomorrow and somehow we're going to give him another hug."

"Allie, do you like Simon as well?" I ask the quieter of the two girls, which is like saying I am asking the uglier of the two supermodels in the *Sports Illustrated* swimsuit issue.

"I like Simon, except when he skis against Tanner," says Allie. "I like Tanner more."

I might forget all of Simon's sponsors, but what I don't forget is that a five-foot-six skier with a boyish face and brown, moppy hair, has fans from Ohio and that I'm trying to convince myself that his story is somehow critical to a book on ski bums, but it is. Johnny Davis, the Face Rats, Keith Erickson, Howie Henderson—they don't have agents. Their skiing doesn't reach more than a million viewers. And they aren't walking billboards. Their reach is the length of their ski poles. Agents don't get involved in anything unless there's lots of money being exchanged and their percentage, usually around fifteen, is worth the work to secure sponsors.

Michael has his own management company, and his client list includes other top skiers like Colby West. The world's top snowboarders, meanwhile, have agents who work for major sports management companies that represent NBA, NFL, and NHL athletes. Shaun White is repped by IMG; Hannah Teter, Danny Kass, and Travis Rice by Octagon. Working for a ski town newspaper, where I wrote stories about teenage pro snowboarders like Lake Tahoe's Jamie Anderson, whose sponsors make it possible for her to buy cars and boats with cash, I already knew that skiing and snowboarding was big business. But it wasn't until that Saturday night in the lobby of the Little Nell hotel in Aspen when I realized that skiing and snowboarding is such big business that their athletes big-time other people.

After four days of being ignored, Michael sets up a brief meeting with Simon, and this one actually happens. Conveniently, Simon is on his way to the big air competition, which he wins easily by performing a Superman double-front flip over a jump taller than most buildings in Aspen. We shake hands in the lobby, he flashes me a wry smile, and then assures me we will talk tonight after the competition. I decide to watch the event on ESPN in the Double Dog, a basement-level bar that serves decent microbrews. When the judging was over,

Simon throws his Salomon skis in front of the camera, but I never hear from him. It's one thing to avoid somebody through intermediary parties, but it's another to look someone in the eye and do it. By Sunday, I give up. He competed in slopestyle that morning, and then immediately drove back to his home in Summit County, Colorado—at least that's what Michael told me. On Monday, I boarded a train from Glenwood Springs to Reno. I returned to work at the *Tahoe Daily Tribune* the following day and was laid off a week later.

Unemployed, I head to Jackson Hole and snowboard. When I am there, Michael e-mails to apologize for what happened in Aspen and convinces me that Simon can meet with me at another event later in the week near Lake Tahoe. It's snowing in Jackson, and I am enjoying fresh powder turns and talking with JHAF members. Against my better judgment, I leave Saturday and drive nearly a thousand miles to Lake Tahoe. On Sunday, I drive through a steady rain along the eastern shore of Lake Tahoe, which means it's snowing at the upper elevations (more powder time being missed), to Northstar-at-Tahoe.

Michael called me that morning and instructed me to call Simon's best friend, Jake, who manages Simon's company, Empire. I called Jake, we exchanged initial pleasantries, and then I told him I was leaving South Lake Tahoe to meet him in an hour to speak with Simon. He told me Simon has an autograph session at 11:00 a.m., but we can talk in his hotel room afterward. I get to the village at Northstar, where Simon is staying. I call Jake, and he doesn't answer. I leave a message. He sends a text message stating that Simon's autograph session has ended but they are eating lunch and will call me when they are through. They never call. I never call back. I never bother telling Michael about this episode.

A few weeks later, Simon Dumont is holding a camera and volunteering as a field correspondent for the *Jim Rome Show* on ESPN. He's reporting from Northstar-at-Tahoe on the day before I was told that he would meet with me. But he wasn't volunteering because he wasn't doing it for altruistic reasons. Before he signs off and thanks Jim Rome, his litany of sponsors has already flashed on the television screen. When ESPN requests Simon, he isn't napping or eating lunch. But when a reporter writing a book on ski bums asks for an interview, he is tired and hungry. I wonder if he will be tired and hungry if, God forbid, something happens to him like what happened to CR Johnson.

In 2005, CR was filming at Brighton Ski Resort outside Salt Lake City. There was one sequence where several skiers were hitting a jump in succession. Trailing behind CR was Kye Petersen, who collided with CR in the air. The collision resulted in a gash above one of CR's eyebrows. The cut only needed three stitches to repair, but the impact knocked him unconscious. He was airlifted to the University of Utah hospital, where he was given sedatives and remained in a comatose state. No big deal. CR's friends figured he'd be skiing again the next week. He remained in a coma for ten days.

Although he was wearing a helmet at the time of the accident, CR experienced major brain trauma. When he awoke from the coma, he was paralyzed. The only movement he had was in his eyes. Within a few weeks, he could sit up in his bed and speak in whispers. At first, he could only respond to questions by blinking. In the several months he spent recovering in the hospital, he had to learn how to swallow, how to eat, how to walk, how to use his arms and legs. He had to re-learn everything. It wasn't the ideal holiday season for the Johnson family, but they received a nice Christmas present when CR started eating solid food again by December 25.

Before the accident, he was primed to take over the skiing

world. In 2002, when he was eighteen, he won a silver medal in his first slopestyle appearance at the Winter X Games. His slopestyle medal was preceded by a bronze-medal finish the previous year in big air. Big air is what separated CR from the rest of the field. The same year he won silver at the Winter X Games, he completed a 1260 (3½ body rotations) in a big air competition at the U.S. Open. The maneuver landed him in the top spot on the podium. He was nominated for Male Skier of the Year at the 2002 ESPN Action Sports and Music Awards, and close friend Tanner Hall started to label CR the best skier in the world. Sponsors followed. CR was just a teenager, but he was considered one of the best skiers in the world and was making crazy amounts of money. The sponsors viewed him as a prodigy, a piece of clay they could mold how they saw fit, and CR obliged. If they said "Jump," he asked "How high?" After all, you don't get far in life telling your bosses no.

Before he was even out of the hospital and just starting to walk after the accident, his career was in shambles.

"I was riding for Salomon [one of Simon's main sponsors], and they dropped me before I was out of the hospital," says CR. "When the word got out, the Internet blew up with people talking shit about Salomon and that move they pulled. I couldn't get them to re-sign me for ten months, and once people started talking bad about them I got a contract for the next two months that also included the time I was hurt. Once that was up, they dropped me officially. Smith Optics has stood behind me 100 percent, 100 percent of the way. They are the best. I love riding for Smith and will for the rest of my time that I ride. Spyder stood behind me at first. Then the company started doing bad and had to cut costs, so they dropped me, blaming my head injury. They had already re-signed me twice, and what they had to say about it was untrue, and so legally that situation is still unfolding. It was perfect though because 4FRNT signed me right away, and working with them is the most encouraging situation I am involved in [right now]."

It's been four years since the accident, though CR was skiing again in 2006. He made an appearance in Matchstick Productions' 2007 film *Seven Sunny Days*, where his recovery was detailed. I watched the film in a casino in Lake Tahoe, and his segment caused people's eyes to tear up. It helped that he was from nearby Truckee since ski towns are supportive of their athletes, but his smile was radiant. It was refreshing to see smiles in ski films. It was like a new person had been born in the same body.

"I want to become the professional skier that I was," CR says in the movie. "Only those things you truly love will you pursue with that energy. For me, my family, and my friends, that's worth dying for.... Throughout the entire process, no doctor, no therapist, and my parents certainly would never let me give up on anything. It's too easy to give up on the things that are hard to accomplish, so I kept trying and kept trying. Everything has come back at an exponential rate. I know it will happen. I am confident it will happen. It will take a little bit of time, and it's going to take a lot of effort and a lot of energy. I will give it that. I have to. I have to because that's what I want for my life, and what I want for my life I am willing to work for. And what I am willing to work for, I am definitely going to achieve."

After showing clips of him throwing tricks off cliffs and falling, his segment ended and the crowd applauded. The applause continued and drowned out the beginning of the next skier's segment. But while the skiing has come back at an exponential rate for CR, the sponsors haven't, and his outlook has changed in the past two years. The entire winter of 2008–9, he was filming for Poor Boyz Productions, one of nearly two dozen film companies that produce annual films these days. His lifestyle isn't the same as it was before the accident, when there was pressure from sponsors, but CR is having fun again, and his skiing is progressing.

"There are still some lingering effects from my accident. My confidence has not come back entirely, which will help my skiing so much when it does. My familiarity with the sport is still a bit shaken. I am having a hard time with line choices, and I react a little slowly to intense situations. I will be my best ever at skiing in the future, but I will always battle with the subconscious fear of being hurt or dying. Overcoming the psychological barrier of injury and death is difficult, especially when you have visited injury and near death. At that point you know the reality and are not just aware of it. For me, I put fair pressure on myself to push my comfort levels, but never to put myself in a dangerous situation. Sometimes sponsors will put pressure on me to perform. Some are worse than others. Some of my companies are happy about my performance and want to see me continue to do better and better, and others just want me to be as good as whichever skier is the best, or I am going to get pay cuts. The companies that put that indirect pressure on me I still work for but am less motivated by. The supportive companies . . . I will work my ass off for, because I appreciate how they are treating me.

"Physically, I have come back stronger than ever, but emotionally I still face an incredible battle. It is hard to ski my best when all parts of me are not working together. The whole process has made me have to step back and ask myself if professional skiing is what I want for my life. Is it worth being hurt? Is it worth dying? Once a person is not on top of the ski world, the industry treats that individual totally different. Things are a little colder and discouraging. I see now that most ski athletes are simply cookies out of the cookie cutter and pursue the same goals. It is important for me to cook my own pie, instead of fighting for the same piece as everyone else. For most young skiers, the idea is to do the next craziest trick and the next biggest spin. At some point, there is only so much humans can do along those lines. At some point most athletes will do certain things because of Kodak courage or sponsor pressure. Some sponsors treat athletes like huck monkeys and don't care if a person gets hurt. If that athlete is finding their motivation from that, it can be a dangerous thing."

According to American Sports Data Inc., the most practical method of assessing risk potential in a sport is to measure the number of injuries per 1,000 athlete exposures—the number of times a participant engages in the activity over the course of a year. If using this method, boxing is the most dangerous with 5.2 injuries per 1,000 exposures, but snowboarding is third (3.8) and skiing is fifth (3.0). According to the National Ski Areas Association, thirty-eight skiers and snowboarders die, on average, each year. The NSAA states that annually there are, on average, forty-two serious injuries, which include paralysis and head injuries. The unfortunate part of skiing and snowboarding is that the better a person gets at skiing and snowboarding, the increased likelihood for a fatality or a serious injury to occur.

In 2009, Shane McConkey, a former *Powder* magazine skier of the year and a poster child for Red Bull energy drink, died when he was unable to deploy his parachute during a free-fall from a cliff in Italy's Dolomite Mountains. According to reports, the film star legend, with more than twenty credits to his name, had performed a double backflip off a 2,000-foot cliff and planned to release his skis and then fly in a wingsuit, something he'd done in previous films for Matchstick Productions. His skis didn't release, and he was killed upon impact. He was thirty-nine and left behind a wife and daughter.

"I once asked him, 'Why are you doing these things?'" Hank de Vre, an adventure photographer who worked with Shane, told journalist Robert Frohlich in an article for *Moonshine Ink*. "'Don't you want to record my demise?' Shane said. I can't help but admit I always scratched my head and worried."

In 2006, Marc-Andre Belliveau, who starred in several TGR films, was on a heli-skiing shoot in British Columbia and stumbled into a field of jagged rocks. He broke his back and was left paralyzed from the waist down. He still skis on a device called a sit-ski, but he is no longer one of freeskiing's rising stars. In 2008, Billy Poole died during a ski accident in Utah while filming for Warren Miller Entertainment. Three months later, John Nicoletta of Aspen died at the World Freeskiing Championships in Alyeska, Alaska. In the TGR movie *Anomaly* a few years earlier, Jamie Pierre set a world record by skiing off a 245-foot cliff at Grand Targhee resort near Jackson. His impact created a deep bomb hole that he eventually skied away from, yet Billy and John died in falls in much more forgiving terrain.

Many skiers criticized Jamie's jump as nothing more than being a test dummy, which CR believes is how many sponsors view skiers and snowboarders. It's one thing for professional skiers and snowboarders to injure themselves in the pursuit of making a living, but it's problematic when they start influencing the younger generation.

In 2005, a few months after CR's accident, South Lake Tahoe's Courtney Royce launched off a jump and glided over a sixty-five-foot gap at Alpine Meadows ski resort. When she landed, her skis slid out from under her, and one popped off. Her lower body bent backward, and her butt slammed into the icy surface. A few hours later, x-rays revealed the impact had crushed 40 percent of her T-12 vertebrae and caused a minor compression fracture in her T-6. The vibration missed splitting her spinal cord by a centimeter, meaning she was one centimeter from being paralyzed like Marc-Andre.

Courtney crushed her vertebrae not in the Winter X Games but in a practice jump before a regional big air competition. She wasn't attempting any rotations. It was a simple, straightforward air, something she had done a hundred times before. The previous winter, Courtney finished thirteenth in moguls and third in halfpipe at the youth national championships. Now doctors say she'll never be 100 percent again. When I visited the sixteen-year-old, she greeted me with a weak handshake and a grimace. She was wearing a plastic back brace and was in obvious pain. She would be in that back brace for several more months, but she never blamed skiing for it.

"There are injuries in every sport," she says. "People are going to get hurt if they are trying new things. A sport is never going to grow if you're worried about getting injured. I think every kid wants to be good. It's one fall. It's not a mistake [her accident]. I don't want to be paralyzed. I think I'll be a little more tentative when I get back. I don't want it to happen again. But in this sport, it's not a question of if a fall will happen but when."

Courtney's father, Tom, shook his head when he heard that.

"There isn't a worse moment for a parent, knowing your kid is in the back of an ambulance, and there's nothing you can do," says Tom, a Face Rat at Heavenly.

Tom showed me his daughter's picture album. On the front cover was a photo of Courtney sandwiched between Tanner and CR. They inspired her. She often visits the Web site newschoolers.com, which has nearly 130,000 registered users, and engages in online discussions about topics such as "Who's better: Simon or Tanner?" But there aren't many discussion threads such as "When will going big ever become too big?" or "How many deaths or snapped spinal cords must occur before skiers start to decide between life and potential stardom?" Sponsors certainly aren't going to be the ones to make that decision or start those threads.

"For sure kids are looking at guys on TV and saying 'Wow, I want to do that, I want to be like that," said Doug Falkanger, Courtney's coach on the Heavenly ski team. "It's progressed so fast. People are becoming such good skiers so fast and doing things that are crazy. We always talk about that, wondering what the sport is going to be like in the future. There's really no way to tell."

Courtney is correct that there are injuries in every sport, but there is something more imminent and certain if something goes wrong flying a sixty-five-foot gap. The risk is enormous, in a much different sense than in football, where a 225-pound linebacker with pads tackles a 225-pound running back with pads. If this type of accident can happen during practice at a regional competition, what might Courtney attempt if the camera is on and her job or next sponsorship deal hinges on the shot?

On February 24, 2010, CR wasn't trying to get the shot. He was just skiing with friends at Squaw Valley, where he fell in a tight section of rocks in the resort's Light Towers area. According to published reports, CR fell face first and then spun around before rocks collided with the back of his head. Ski patrol arrived on the scene and attempted to revive him. He was wearing a helmet, but it didn't matter. County medical personnel said he died upon impact. He was twenty-six.

I had developed a special affinity for CR for the same reasons I did with Johnny Davis. Like me, both had cheated death or impairment in their twenties. And like most professional skiers and snowboarders, he was tough to nail down for a face-to-face interview. However, he never stopped trying, which meant he had something to say. With my deadline looming, we were ultimately forced to converse on social networking Web site Facebook. He was candid and forthright in his responses. As a ski town journalist for nearly a decade, countless pro skiers and snowboarders have danced around my questions about the nefarious side of the winter sports industry. CR didn't. He willingly discussed the industry's cutthroat nature. After what he had gone through following his first skiing accident that left him in a coma, he wasn't naïve enough to believe there wasn't another side to the industry. He was also mature enough to speak his mind when it might have negatively affected his career. That takes courage.

In the days following his death, hundreds of fans, friends, and family members left messages for CR on his Facebook page. There was a wide range of emotional responses, but most people knew him to be genuine, inspirational, and one of the best skiers in the world. That's a pretty nice way to be remembered.

It's a blurred line and certainly not a universal one, but the point when professional skiers are no longer ski bums is when sponsors begin influencing the progression of the sport, not the people who began to ski and snowboard for, as JK put it, the love of the game. TGR's Corey Gavitt admits that there are unfortunate realities that have happened because of the rapid progression of skiing and snowboarding, and that the symbiotic relationship between competitions, film companies, and sponsors affects the purity of the industry. His response? It is what it is.

"Hey, you don't get in our films without having to eat dirt," says Corey Gavitt. "You don't get this good—you don't get in X Games—without loving skiing and being a ski bum. You put your work in and ski a hundred days a year. There is no other way. And if what we do helps skiers and snowboarders get out

of restaurants and make a living from skiing and snowboarding, I think that's a good thing because, let me tell you, I've
worked as a server and I have no desire to do it again. Micah
worked as a dishwasher, and I don't think he wants to forget
about his sponsors—sponsors that have given him a great life
and inspired kids all around the world to go ski—and go back
to washing dishes. If Rossignol wants to help Sage—and Sage
wants to help Rossignol—that's helping the sport. And let's be
real. We might be influencing the younger culture and making
them think they can make tons of money from skiing, but it's
like basketball. Everybody dreams of being in the NBA, but how
many kids actually make it? One percent, maybe? It's no different in skiing. There is a natural progression in everything,
and maybe this is it for the ski bum and skiing in general. In
Jackson, there are locals who are awesome skiers, probably
better than some of the athletes in our films, but they don't
want to stand on a windy ridge for an hour while we set up
cameras. They don't want to radio in what line they are going
to do. They don't want to spend powder days filming. They
just want to go out and ski, and thank God for that because
this is our job, and it's not a job for everyone. Our guys put
their lives on the line, whether it's in competitions or filming.
They should be taken care of financially, and I am not going
to judge anybody who's trying to make a living."

It was at that moment, sitting across from Corey in a dim
room, years after talking with Johnny Davis and Keith Erickson
and the Face Rats, when I knew something was amiss. Corey
and Todd chewed tobacco during our conversations, their
bottom lip cavities were always filled with chaw. Occasionally
they stopped talking long enough to spit into a plastic bottle,
and I rarely noticed the dribble that oozed toward the curl of
their chins. I rarely noticed such dribble, not because I was
mesmerized with what they were telling me, but because I

was baffled by what we were talking about; the topic of our conversations, not the specifics of them. As Corey spoke, his words become muted and I thought of Johnny Davis and the initial conversation we had in Portland, Oregon, in that coffee shop with vanilla walls. Corey stopped talking and was out of chaw, and I was out of questions and left.

I leaned against the blue handle of the Teton Gravity Research office door and it flung open into the Wyoming winter. I slid my left hand along the blue railing that parallels the metal grated staircase until I was near the picnic bench outside the Village Café. I looked up and noticed the sky had turned silver, like tinfoil placed underneath a lamp. I continued walking toward the parking lot. It never occurred to me to look back. By the time I reached my car, it was snowing. They were small flakes, nothing too exciting, but I knew in Jackson that someone was waxing their skis and would be waking up at 5:00 a.m. the next morning because they wanted first box. And if there is only one person left who does that, isn't that enough? Yeah, maybe it's not the way it used to be, but maybe it never was.

Epilogue

The definition of purity is something that is unaffected, but nothing remains unaffected. My dream is that this book becomes inaccurate down the road, that the American empire crumbles and rebuilds itself on bricks whose integrity isn't defined by money. I dream that the younger generation, which will ultimately decide ski bum culture in fifty years, watches ski and snowboard movies and reads magazines, and it stokes a desire to ditch traditional ways of life and seek a life in the mountains for the right reasons. But I know better. Even young people living in ski towns who have adopted ski bum principles in a modernized ski town don't want to be called ski bums. It used to be a term of endearment in ski towns, a badge of honor.

"I am not a ski bum," Travis McDowell told the *Jackson Hole News and Guide*. "Maybe we should rename the whole phenomenon and call ourselves enlightened. People work all year to take two weeks off and do what we do."

Nowadays, we just tolerate and judge the various levels of pollution. Sure, ski bums could rise up and rage against the machine, but they're too busy skiing, as they should be. Everything in life is fluid, and all moments are fleeting. I once wrote in the *Tahoe Daily Tribune* that the sequel is never the same as the original. Whenever there is a break in the river, the water always flows a little differently after that. For ski bums, one's time on earth should be reduced to one fundamental element: Enjoy life. The search for powder can be anything for anyone. Just enjoy life since you only have one. That's their motto, and I understand it. When I am seventy years old and holding my grandchild on my lap, rocking back and forth on a chair, I want to be able to tell the story of my river. And, of course, the more places it meandered along the way—the more times I enjoyed life—should make for a better story.

Bibliography

Castle, Ken. *Heavenly Dreams*. Park City UT: Park City Publishing, 2005.

Clifford, Hal. *Downhill Slide: Why the Corporate Ski Industry is Bad for Skiing, Ski Towns, and the Environment*. San Francisco: Sierra Club Books, 2002.

Forstenzer, Martin. *Mammoth: The Sierra Legend*. Boulder CO: Mountain Sports Press, 2002.

Gonzales, David. *Jackson Hole: On a Grand Scale*. Boulder CO: Mountain Sports Press, 2002.

Klaczkiewicz, Jon. *Swift, Silent, Deep*. DVD. Directed by Jon Klaczkiewicz. Wilson WY: SSD Productions, LLC, 2009.

Sykes, Hunter, and Darren Campbell. *Resorting to Madness: Taking Back Our Mountain Communities*. DVD. Olympic Valley CA: Coldstream Creative, 2006.

Gersh, Jeff, and Chelsea Congdon. *Subdivide and Conquer: A Modern Western*. DVD. Oley PA: Bullfrog Films, 1999.

CPSIA information can be obtained
at www.ICGtesting.com
Printed in the USA
LVHW04s0710040518
575780LV00001B/1/P